Do any of these sound familiar?

- Taking your kid's guff and sass is all part of an average day, like drinking coffee at 7:00 a.m.
- Naptime is for you *and* your toddler, or he won't rest.
- After you cook your daughter's favorite dinner, she changes her mind about what she likes.
- You can predict the sibling fights—the order, the exact phrases, and even the timing—before your youngest yells, "Mom, she's picking on me!"
- You've become a WWE pro just to get your kids in bed. Problem is, they don't stay there.
- Your mood swings match your adolescent drama queen's.
- "But I can't do it—it's too hard!" is a well-worn mantra in your house.
- When you fight, your child wins, because you're the one who feels guilty.
- You're used to a monkey-like appendage around your legs every time you walk through the kindergarten door.
- You don't even wince at slamming bedroom doors anymore.
- You frequently get caught in your child's tornado-like winds.
- One of your kids is like a no-see-um—constantly flying around, biting you, and irritating you.
- You have one child you have to placate or tiptoe around.
- You're better at doing your child's chores than he is.
- She has nothing to wear, and it's *your fault*.
- He's pitched so many fits in Walmart, you're too embarrassed to go there anymore.

- You have to lean over nearly parallel to the floor to hear her whisper.
- Your kids' alarm clock is you, you, and you.
- Your four-year-old just tweeted.
- Your teenager thinks gaming is an inalienable right that exists before homework.

If anything above rings a bell, you need this book. I'll reveal not only why kids misbehave but how you can turn that behavior around with practical, no-nonsense strategies that really work . . . *and* are a long-term win for both of you.

By the end of this book, you'll be smiling at the transformation in yourself, your child, *and* your home.

Guaranteed.

Why
Your Kids
Misbehave—and
What to Do
about It

Why Your Kids
Misbehave—

What to Do
about It

DR. KEVIN LEMAN

Revell

a division of Baker Publishing Group
Grand Rapids, Michigan

© 2020 by KAL Enterprises

Published by Revell
a division of Baker Publishing Group
PO Box 6287, Grand Rapids, MI 49516-6287
www.revellbooks.com

Printed in the United States of America

Library of Congress Cataloging-in-Publication Data
Names: Leman, Kevin, author.
Title: Why your kids misbehave—and what to do about it / Dr. Kevin Leman.
Description: Grand Rapids : Revell, a division of Baker Publishing Group, 2020.
Identifiers: LCCN 2019027437 | ISBN 9780800734701 (cloth)
Subjects: LCSH: Child psychology.
Classification: LCC BF721 .L4627 2020 | DDC 155.4—dc23
LC record available at https://lccn.loc.gov/2019027437

ISBN 978-0-8007-3835-8 (ITPE)

20 21 22 23 24 25 26   7 6 5 4 3 2 1

To all you smart parents
who picked up this book.

The knowledge you'll glean
will save
countless future heartaches.

Contents

Acknowledgments

Grateful thanks to:

My Revell team.

My longtime editor Ramona Tucker, who by now can read me like a book.

Introduction

Why Your Kids Work You

Your kids can read you like a book,
and they're master readers.

My lovely wife, Sande, our daughter Krissy, and I recently had dinner at Texas Roadhouse, a favorite steakhouse. Not too far from us was a young couple with Grandma, Grandpa, Auntie, and a cherub in one of those little wooden high chairs at the end of the table. Clearly that 13-month-old didn't want to stay in that high chair prison.

Oh, this is gonna be good, I thought.

The 13-month-old fussed and wriggled in the chair for a few minutes until she was too loud to ignore any longer. Then Dad picked up baby, put her on his lap, and offered her a spoonful of her mac and cheese.

I could predict what was going to happen next . . . and it did.

Baby grabbed the spoon and, with a petite shove of her right fist, sent that mac and cheese flying about a foot, barely missing landing in the middle of Grandma's filet mignon dinner plate.

Eagle-eyed Mom spotted what was going on and reached for baby. "Honey, do you want this? Or do you want that?" she asked, pointing to her own food.

I started chuckling.

Sande and Krissy simultaneously shot me "the look." The one I know from experience means, "Leemie/Dad, don't you even think about it."

So, in deference to my own family members and our cooked-just-right steak, I bit my tongue. I didn't say anything to that cute, well-meaning couple who likely thought they were doing everything right but were, in fact, doing everything wrong. They were already being controlled by a kid who was shorter than a yardstick and likely couldn't even walk yet.

Without intervention of some kind—like carrying out the practical, smart strategies I'll reveal in this book—that same kid will become a mouthy middle-schooler. That mouthy middle-schooler will morph into an uncontrollable teenager with princess syndrome.

Yet those parents who were smiling at their firstborn Snookums had no idea they were on the way to creating a power-driven child.

You see, if you're a parent, you're also the teacher of a daily workshop for your kids, no matter how young or old they are. It's called "How to Misbehave."

Give yourself some credit. You're an awesome teacher. You're adept at balancing trying to do things right in parenting and accepting all kinds of advice from Grandma, Dad, your sister, and even your brother, who isn't a parent yet but thinks he knows best how to handle your little Snookums.

You've read a bunch of parenting books and mommy blogs galore. You've dialogued with other parents in the trenches about a score of hot subjects, such as getting your kid to try new food, how to effectively potty train, the best ways to adapt to kindergarten, how to find a good soccer league, what to take to summer camp, how to navigate a certain teacher known for being a stickler, and which AP classes your child should take or which clubs she should join to ease her way into the university of your choice.

It doesn't matter that your kid isn't even a toddler yet. You're determined to know all the ropes and be a good parent to create a successful child who stands head and shoulders above the rest in every area.

So, in search of the "Parent of the Year" title, you try out all sorts of ideas on your child (aka guinea pig), especially if this is your first go-round in parenting. Some of those brainstorms work, but others don't have a high success rate. *Why is that?* you wonder. They seem to work for other people you read about.

The biggest problem is that, as you find your way in the real-life maze of parenting, you're inconsistent. You try one thing, then another. What does that inconsistency say to the child watching you?

Let's say your child is that 13-month-old I observed at Texas Roadhouse. Take a peek at the "aha" phenomenon going on in her pint-sized brain as her parents interact with her. That smart baby has already put two and two together to come up with, well, four.

Aha 1: Oh, I get it now. I know exactly how to make those people, who look like giants to me, do what I want. I cry, and they pick me up. Simple.

Aha 2: This being a kid isn't as hard as I thought it would be. I give my Cheerios a push off the tray here, and they come running. Look how much power I've got in my little finger.

Aha 3: Gosh, I thought adults would be tough. But these guys are so easy. All I have to do is pout and refuse to open my mouth when they feed me. The next bite they'll offer me comes fully loaded with entertainment—an airplane motion and buzzing noise. I wonder what else I can do to get them to perform like well-trained seals?

Aha 4: So, what's on the menu today? . . . Oh, yuck, it's that squishy mac and cheese again. I hate that stuff. I know. If I launch that spoon back in Dad's face, he'll pass me to Mom, who'll give in and feed me from her plate. At least her food has interesting textures, even if it doesn't always taste good. Even better, I get to sit on her warm lap instead of this cold, hard high chair. And Grandma plays with me then too. I like the googly faces she makes. They make me laugh.

Kids do read us like a book. They're expert readers, in fact, even by the age of 13 months.

Why do kids misbehave? What do *we* have to do with it? And how can we stop that behavior before it starts, or turn the train of misbehavior around when it's already chugging down the path?

There's something called training. It's not only for kids. It's for parents too. *Why Your Kids Misbehave—and What to Do about It*:

- provides expert insight into why kids do what they do and why you do what you do
- explores the basics of what discipline really is and isn't, and why punishment never works
- reveals the four stages of misbehavior and how you can handle each one . . . *before* it progresses
- gives time-tested strategies that have worked with millions of parents and families

- offers real questions from other parents in the trenches and my winning answers

Simply stated, kids work you *because they can.* Those cute ones shorter than a Canada goose? They're smarter than you think. And the gangly ones with big puppy feet and hands who now tower over you at age 14? They've got parental manipulation down pat. But they all have the same agenda—to win you over so they can have what they want, when they want it, and the way they want it. They're programmed to do it from babyhood on, unless you, wise parent, intervene.

However, you already have the upper hand, even if you don't know it. Those kids need you, though they may not act like it and would never admit it. After all, without you they wouldn't even have undies, much less clean ones. Nor would they have any of those gadgets they consider necessary to life, like an iPhone, a smart TV, available transportation, or a refrigerator that's open 24/7.

That's a good starting point for your parental authority, wouldn't you agree?

Why Your Kids Do What They Do

---

*Everything has a beginning,
and so does misbehavior.*

Every parent runs into a few snags as they rear ankle-biters through the hormone group. So if any of these next scenes sound even vaguely familiar, congratulations. You're in good company.

1. Your two-year-old reaches her pinkie into the electrical outlet on the wall five times in one morning. Fearing a zap will scare her or shorten her life span, you're worn out from racing across the room to stop her.

2. Your three-year-old gets kicked out of preschool for yanking toys away from other kids and making them cry. This is the highly coveted preschool you signed up for the month after you gave birth because the waiting list was three years.

3. Your five-year-old princess has a new favorite behavior: stomping her foot and yelling "No!" when you ask her to get dressed for kindergarten in the clothes you've laid out for her.

4. The school office calls you in the middle of a meeting at work to say your six-year-old has been accused of bullying another first-grader. That student's angry parents are waiting for you in the principal's office right now.

5. Your spacey eight-year-old continually leaves a string of possessions outside to get rained on, and you're always playing pickup.

6. When your nine-year-old has math homework, everyone in the family runs for cover. As soon as she wails, "It's too hard!" and starts her crying jag, your night is ruined. You end up doing her homework.

7. Your 10-year-old is such a cranky mess every time he returns from staying at your ex's apartment for the weekend that you wish you could FedEx him back there until he's an adult.

8. Your 11-year-old has mastered picking on his little sister and exiting stage left before you catch him in the act.

9. Your 13-year-old has morphed overnight into an alien creature who talks back.

10. A teacher caught your 14-year-old smoking an aromatic illegal substance in the alleyway behind school. Now your tarnished-wings angel is stuck at home on a month of probation. To him, it seems like a vacation, and he's taking advantage of it. But you? You feel like the one on the hot seat with the school administration, plus you're suffering at home with your bored troublemaker.

11. After taking the keys of the family car without permission, your 15-year-old went for a joyride, got into a fender

bender, and ended up at the police station. He had his rights read to him by a stern police officer and experienced being cuffed and placed in the back of a police car. Then you got a call and had to join the not-so-fun discussion with that police officer at the station.

12. Your 17-year-old isn't getting around to her college applications, so you secretly start to do them because you're afraid she'll miss the application window.

Some of these misbehaviors may seem minor and not worth your attention. After all, you've got a full-time job on top of being a parent and a lot of other worries that keep you up at night, like the washer that needs to be replaced and the leak under your kitchen sink. Surely the little things your kid does that temporarily drive you crazy will pass, right? You'll both feel different in the morning after you get some needed sleep.

However, some of these behaviors demand your immediate attention since people outside your family clan are involved, like a principal or the stern-looking police officer who has your child in tow.

But whether minor or major, all of the above are misbehaviors, and all of them happen for a reason.

Why Misbehavior Continues

Misbehavior will continue happening and will likely grow larger until you identify the underlying reason for that behavior.

That two-year-old who stuck her finger in the electrical outlet? She became the eight-year-old who left her backpack and schoolbooks out in the rain.

That three-year-old who yanked toys away from others at preschool? He became the six-year-old who bullied another child in first grade.

That nine-year-old who cried every time she had to do math? She's now the 17-year-old who can't do her own college applications.

That 11-year-old who picked on his sister, then hightailed it out of Dodge before he got caught? Well, that was only the beginning of the wild rodeo rides he took his parents on, including a joyride in the family car at age 15.

The best thing you can do right now is to envision what kind of adult you want your child to be. One who is responsible and accountable for his actions? One who is respectful, loving and kind toward others, and well-grounded in values important to you? One who has healthy self-worth, has internal motivation to do his best, and contributes in a positive way to his family, neighborhood, and community?

> *Envision what kind of adult you want your child to be.*

No matter where you and your child are right now in your relationship, there's no better time than the present to begin that transformation. It starts with a simple statement: "I want to see some things change around here. For that to happen, we need to do some things differently."

Note the "we" language. There's no finger-pointing at your child. No "*You're* the problem. What's wrong with you? You need to change. You need to stop this behavior."

There's no finger-pointing at yourself. No "I know it's my fault. If only I would have done X, we wouldn't be at this place today."

The past is just that—the past. Nothing good comes from digging up old bones from the backyard and dragging them onto the front porch for viewing. The present, and where you go from this juncture, is what matters.

Both of you are in this relationship. Your job throughout this book is to work on the areas in which the two of you intersect, so that when situations of misbehavior arise, you'll naturally start to think:

What did I do or say in the past?

Well, I . . .

Did that work?

No. It only made the situation worse.

*So what could I do or say differently this time for a better
long-term outcome?*

Let me set your mind at ease. There's no such thing as a perfect parent or a perfect kid, so throw those ideas out the window
right now. Each of you will make mistakes as you go through life,
especially with each other. We tend to unleash our emotions on
those closest to us, because they feel the safest.

It's like the cartoon I saw many years ago that was so true to
life it lodged in my brain. It went something like this:

Dad has a very bad day at work. He walks in the kitchen door and
yells at his wife.

A question mark erupts in thought bubbles as she wonders,
What did I do? Now she's having a bad day. The instant her son
walks in the door, she lets him have it.

The son has two question marks in thought bubbles. *What's
with Mom? She's mad about that old thing?* Now he's having a bad
day. He seeks out his younger brother and picks a fight.

Three question marks erupt in thought bubbles from the
younger brother. *What did I do to deserve this? He could have
gotten me for all kinds of things last week, but I haven't done
anything lately. What's with him?* Now he's having a bad day. He
seeks out the family dog and gives it a swift kick.

Multiple question marks fill the thought bubbles from the dog
as it slinks away to hide behind the couch.

See what I mean? We all have our flawed moments, and we're
inherent experts at passing those moments on to those we love.
So consider that you and your kids are on a shared learning curve.

Your goal in this book is not to get yourself elected for "Mother of the Year" or "Father of the Year." It's not to train your kids to high-jump over the bar of perfectionism either.

Instead, you're going to discover how to walk *together* through life, jumping over whatever hurdles are put in your path, even running side by side when you need to. All with the end goal of transforming your children into the best adults they can be as you stay in healthy authority over them.

> We all have our flawed moments, and we're inherent experts at passing those moments on to those we love.

But don't forget to stop every once in a while to smell the roses.

As the father of five who are now adults, trust me when I say the length of time your children are at home, safely in your nest, is much shorter than you can imagine. That means every minute you have with them is critically important to their long-term welfare and success.

Thinking of any current misbehavior as "bad," or thinking of your child as "being bad" and hoping he'll grow out of it, won't get you anywhere. Instead, treat that current misbehavior as what it is: behavior that you need to work on as a team. Do that and you'll be less likely to react in a heated manner and more likely to respond in a way that's beneficial long-term to your relationship.

Parenting misbehaving kids is never easy. We all have moments when our fuses are short and swiftly lit. But misbehaviors only grow if you don't address them now or you address them incorrectly. I assure you any short-term pain will be worth the long-term gain.

It is possible to channel all that energy from negative behavior in a positive direction if you know a few secrets about why your kids do what they do. So let's start with the most important, basic concept that will revolutionize the way you think about and approach your child's misbehavior.

Purposive Behavior

Of all the words you've used today, this week, or this year, I'll bet you a million bucks you haven't used this one—*purposive.*

Am I right?

Purposive behavior is a psychological term derived from the individual psychology of psychiatrist Alfred Adler.[1] Basically it means all social behavior serves a specific purpose. Everything has a beginning. Children and teenagers are much smarter than you give them credit for. They wouldn't do what they do, and continue doing it, without gaining something from that behavior. Their behavior—including misbehavior—serves a purpose. Simply stated, it works.

But what difference does knowing the term *purposive behavior* mean to you in your real world, when faced with your misbehaving kids who are embarrassing you in front of the neighbors or Granny at Walmart?

Flash back to the situations at the beginning of this chapter, which are based on real-life problems that parents like you have faced. Let's look at the behavior in each situation and identify what purpose it serves to answer the question, Why does the child do that or keep doing that?

Behavior #1: Your two-year-old keeps sticking her finger in the electrical outlet.

Purpose it serves: The answer is simple. That action gets you, Mom, to pay attention to her. Even more, you run toward her like a crazy person, and you're awfully entertaining. It's better than the cartoon movie she watches when you're busy.

Why wouldn't your cherub play this game over and over? It's a doubleheader: attention *and* entertainment.

> *Why wouldn't your cherub play this game over and over? It's a doubleheader: attention and entertainment.*

Behavior #2: Your three-year-old gets kicked out of a highly coveted preschool for yanking toys away from other kids and making them cry.

Purpose it serves: He got his teacher's attention . . . more than his fair share, in fact. Out of all those kids in the room, he made the teacher keep her eye on him.

Going from home, where he had all of the attention, to a place where he had to fight to be noticed because there were a lot more kids like him—who couldn't tie their shoes either—wasn't so hard anymore.

Behavior #3: Your five-year-old princess stomps her foot and yells "No!" when you ask her to get dressed for kindergarten in the clothes you've laid out for her.

Purpose it serves: Her loud defiance gets your attention fast. She doesn't want to go to kindergarten because it's a noisy place, and she's an only child used to having and creating noise only when she wants it. Also, kindergarten is a scary place with a lot of kids like her, when she's used to being top dog at home. Add to that the fact she doesn't like the scratchy collared shirt you make her wear because you noticed all of the other girls are wearing something like it.

Saying "no" leads you to cajole her into going, which takes a while, so you're often late to school. By then most of the kindergarteners are already in their seats, quietly working. She doesn't have to jostle for her place among the other kids who are hanging up their jackets and backpacks on the hooks. As a bonus, somewhere along the way you gave up and allowed her to wear the shirt she wanted, just to get her out the door.

Score: Kid 3, Mom 0.

Behavior #4: The school office calls to say your six-year-old is bullying another first-grader, and that child's parents and the principal are waiting for you.

Purpose it serves: Your hackles rise with immediate attention, right in the middle of that work meeting. Half of you is angry with your kid for getting into this situation. The other half is in full Mama/Papa Bear mode: "How are you sure *my* kid did it? Did you see him do it? He isn't the kind to do this. How do you know the other kid didn't provoke him first?"

You've been so busy in your new job that you haven't had much time to listen to your son talk about how first grade is going in his new school, or to show up for the open house, where kids performed a play for the parents. But now you're in gather-information mode at your battle-command station, and you're armed and loaded.

Behavior #5: Your spacey eight-year-old continually leaves a string of possessions outside to get rained on, and you're always playing pickup.

Purpose it serves: That eight-year-old may act spacey, but she's certainly not dumb. She's got you trained like a circus animal. She knows you like items in their rightful place and you especially hate it when possessions get lost or unnecessarily ruined because people don't take care of them.

Leaving her backpack to get soaked in the rain is a ploy for your attention. Even if you're busy getting dinner ready and don't stop to talk to her for very long, as soon as you see that backpack outside, out you go to retrieve it.

What you don't see is her lurking around the corner, laughing every time you do it.

Then again, some kids are naturally lazy or spacey, even if you didn't go out and snowplow their roads. Not everything a child does is tied to the purposive nature of life. Sometimes they're only being who they are.

Behavior #6: When your nine-year-old has math homework, everyone in the family runs for cover. As soon as she wails, "It's too hard!" and starts her crying jag, your night is ruined. You end up doing her homework.

Purpose it serves: There's nothing like a kid wailing, "But it's too hard! I can't do it!" to get a parent's attention. Especially if it comes with a bucketload of tears and a slamming bedroom door.

But that nine-year-old is working you. She doesn't feel like doing her homework, and she's angling for you to do it for her. It works. You fall into her trap every time. See why the misbehavior continues?

Behavior #7: Your 10-year-old is such a cranky mess every time he returns from your ex's apartment that you wish you could FedEx him back until he's an adult.

Purpose it serves: He's so irritable that he makes you pay attention to him, even if his behavior provokes negative comments like, "Go to your room . . . and don't come out until you have a better attitude."

> There's nothing like a kid wailing, "But it's too hard! I can't do it!" to get a parent's attention. Especially if it comes with a bucketload of tears and a slamming bedroom door.

For your son, even negative attention is better than the *nada* attention he gets at his dad's place. Your ex-husband has a new wife and a whiny two-year-old who everybody thinks is cute. As far as your son is concerned, he might as well blend into the walls. He even has to rummage in the fridge when he's hungry because everybody eats around the toddler's schedule or their own work schedules. There's no family dinner table there, like he's used to with you, or when the three of you were a family. He's been living on leftover cold pizza for the past two days.

Your son's brain is extra busy as he walks through your door every weekend. He wonders, *Why do I have to be there if nobody even cares that I'm there? And why do I have to sleep on their office couch with all their stuff, when I have my own bedroom at home with all my stuff? Just because of some dumb court ruling? At least Mom talks to me, warms food up for me, eats with me, and notices I'm home.*

But you don't hear those thoughts. Nor do you recognize that his bad attitude is a call for you, the person he cares about the most and knows cares about him the most, to give him what he didn't have for the weekend: attention. All you can see is a sulky, angry kid who seems determined to pick on you every time he returns home.

Behavior #8: Your 11-year-old has mastered picking on his little sister and exiting stage left before you catch him in the act.

Purpose it serves: Your 11-year-old is a genius, no doubt about it. He knows there's no better way to get your attention than to pick on the "helpless" baby of the family. Not to mention it's also fun to create some drama since her responding squeal is so predictable in his unpredictable, dog-eat-dog adolescent world. It's like a magician learning how to pull the exact item out of his hat that makes the audience applaud and respond, "Oh, wow."

He may not be at the top of the food chain at school, but at home he's the master of the show. The fact that your magician exits as soon as his sister yells, "Mom!" shows he knows exactly what behavior to expect from you.

> *There's no better way to get your attention than to pick on the "helpless" baby of the family.*

He's smart enough to stay out of reach of those flailing arms in your initial reaction. All he gets is your cooled-down later version as you say, hands on hips, "Young man, I expect more from you because you're older . . ."

He goes back to his room, grinning because the show he created worked. Your attention to his misbehavior drives him to scheme how next to torture his sister.

Let the games continue.

Behavior #9: Your 13-year-old has morphed overnight into an alien creature who talks back.

Purpose it serves: Your shocked expression says it all. You might have been focused on cleaning out the basement, but *now* you're paying attention. How could the sweet child who loved to curl up by your side and wanted to hold your hand at the grocery store be acting like this?

By getting your attention through sass, your new teenager is saying, "Hey, look at me. I'm changing. I'm not exactly comfortable with how I'm changing. Sometimes I still want to be a little kid, and I really need my mom and dad. Other times I think they're the stupidest people on the planet. Sometimes I want to be a grown-up, and I'm tired of adults telling me what to do. And sometimes I don't like myself—my body parts are getting weird—or know what I want. I need help, but I don't know how to ask for it, and I'm not sure if I want it. I'm kind of mixed up."

Well, that's the understatement of the century. Adolescents can be more changeable in emotional color than chameleons faced with imminent danger.

Welcome to the hormone group, you lucky parent, you.

Behavior #10: A teacher caught your 14-year-old smoking an aromatic illegal substance in the alleyway behind school, but it feels like you're the one on the hot seat with the school and suffering at home.

Purpose it serves: After a forced move due to your job relocation and leaving all his childhood friends behind, your 14-year-old has been decidedly unhappy. He found a way to let you know how unhappy he is and that it's all *your* fault. That's why he didn't work as hard as his new friends to flee the scene, so he was the only one caught. Because he wouldn't give up the names of his new posse smoking with him, he's the one who got the time.

The cryptic phone call from school and the probation sentence got your attention, all right. Not only do you look like a bad parent in this new small town, but the school administration has already labeled your kid as a troublemaker. And your teenager is working hard to find new ways to make you suffer at home, including turning your house into a pigsty while you're at work and refusing to do anything you ask him to.

He found a way to let you know how unhappy he is and that it's all your fault.

Behavior #11: After taking the keys of the family car without permission, your 15-year-old went for a joyride, got into a fender bender, and ended up at the police station.

Purpose it serves: Your teenager has been bugging you to give him more time behind the wheel on his driver's permit, but you've been busy with . . . well, life in general. He has more than half of his driving hours in, and he still has six months to go before he turns 16 and could even go for his license. But he's impatient and doesn't think you take him seriously.

When he asked you earlier to go driving with him, you had a deadline to finish, so you said, "No, not tonight. We can practice driving on Saturday and Sunday."

You could sense the heavy eye roll even with your back turned. Then again, you're used to it. You've got two teenagers.

Since that timeline sounded like a lifetime away, and your son couldn't get your attention when he wanted it and how he wanted it, he took matters into his own hands. He sneaked the car keys off the hook by the back door and took control of his own destiny with a joyride to pick up a friend a few miles away. They'd only intended to pick up some food at a local drive-through, but then he couldn't resist flooring it at an intersection.

Now that dinged car bumper is the least of your worries. He's lost his beginner's permit, and you've lost any shred of a sense of humor.

Behavior #12: Your 17-year-old isn't getting around to her college applications, so you secretly start to do them because you're afraid she'll miss the application window.

Purpose it serves: What a smart teenager. All that online paperwork is daunting, and she really doesn't want to do it. She knows that if she grabs your attention and sympathy by looking super busy and stressed by her classes and looming life transitions, you'll rescue her. After all, if someone else will do it, why should she? It gives her a lot more time to text her friends, buy new songs on iTunes, and watch crazy cat clips on YouTube.

The Secret Your Kids Don't Want You to Know

As we looked at each of those behaviors, did you see how every single behavior served a purpose in that child's life? Let's be blunt. If *you* did a certain action and it served a purpose that was beneficial to you, wouldn't you want to continue doing it?

Of course you would. So would I. As the baby of the family, I learned early on that if I didn't feel like doing something, I only had to drag my feet until my older brother and older sister were either told to do it by my parents or did it anyway because they, as perfectionists, couldn't stand that thing not being done.

Why did I do that? Because it worked.

Why do you do a certain action now? Because it works.

For example, you love cooking but hate cleaning up. You purposefully don't allow enough time to clean up before you have to leave for your long-awaited night out with friends. You know your neatnik partner won't be able to stand it, so he'll clean up for you . . . even if he's muttering the whole time. As long as he cleans up, that's beneficial to you, right?

But what if you made a mess and came home to that same mess? And no one stepped in to clean it up for you? You might be swayed to clean it up before it solidifies into cement on your kitchen counter and you have to scrub harder. Delaying cleanup would no longer be beneficial in your life.

So here's the secret your child doesn't want you to know: his misbehavior will continue as long as it's beneficial in his life. When it no longer gains him anything, he'll stop. If it's an ingrained behavior, it might take a few times for him to get into his noggin that the picture is changing. But don't worry. Eventually he'll get it, and his behavior will change.

In all 12 scenarios we examined—composites of real-life situations—the misbehavior started at the beginning because of a single word. That's why I've used that key word on purpose in every single scenario. Did you happen to spot it?

If you're a detailed person (likely a firstborn, by the way), you probably did, and it might even have annoyed you a bit. *Why can't a person with "Dr." in front of their name come up with a different word for that?*

If you're a middleborn, you might have noticed, but it didn't bother you. After all, you're along for the ride in figuring out how to juggle being your child's parent *and* friend.

If you're the baby of the family, you're breezing through the book and hitting the highlights (or asking your firstborn partner or friend to read the book for you and give you the highlights), so you didn't even notice that overused word.

So what is that word?

A-*T-T-E-N-T-I-O-N*.

I even spelled it out for you to get *your* attention.

That, dear parents, is exactly what those misbehaving kids are doing to you. Why you in particular? Read on.

Why You—and Only You—Will Do

*Why your child wants your attention,
needs your attention, and was
programmed to fall in love with you.*

Kids are as social as sea lions on a rock on a beautiful sunny day in Monterey, California. If you pay attention to them—clapping for them, appreciating their antics—they'll perform all kinds of tricks and slap their fins happily.

But wait. Turn your back, ignore them, or get busy with something else, and you're the one in trouble. First they'll call more loudly for attention. Then they'll splash you in a mini power play. If those milder ways don't work, they might try a bit of sea lion revenge. I've seen a sea lion snitch a sun hat from a woman who was sitting on a nearby rock. Another sneaked up on a man who was sleeping and nudged him so hard he slid off the ledge into the ocean.

Kids, like sea lions, perform to get attention. And the attention they want most of all? Yours. Even if it seems like their body language is saying, "Get out of my space," they want you in it. Even when they rail against any "rules" you set, those boundaries create a safety net for them.

> Kids, like sea lions, perform to get attention. And the attention they want most of all? Yours.

Outwardly they might be rolling their eyes or saying, "C'mon, really?" But inwardly they're sighing with relief. *Yeah, things are tough right now. But I'm okay. Mom and Dad care about me, so everything's going to turn out all right.*

That's why how *you* respond to any of your child's misbehaviors is key.

Imprinting on You

Did you know that your child, from the very beginning, was programmed to fall in love with you?

When an infant first opens her eyes, what she sees leaves a lasting impression. This process is known as *imprinting*. The idea of imprinting goes all the way back to 1873 and an English biologist, Douglas Spalding, who noted that baby chicks followed the first moving object they saw. He called this the *stamping in* of an impression.

This stamping-in process was later called *imprinting* by a German biologist, Oskar Heinroth, but it was his student, the Austrian ornithologist Konrad Lorenz, who popularized the idea by studying mother-baby bonding with geese. Lorenz removed the mother, artificially incubated the eggs, and ensured that *he* was the first moving object the babies saw when they hatched. The result? Those babies followed *him* around as if he was their mother. It didn't matter that he didn't even vaguely resemble a goose.

Lorenz's groundbreaking experiment revealed how critical the presence of a mother figure is for baby geese. Simply stated, recognizing "Mama" gives youngsters "a survival advantage in understanding who they can trust and where food can be obtained from."[2]

Without Mama, baby geese couldn't survive in the wild.

If It Quacks Like a Duck, It Might Not Be One

Way back when I was first studying psychology at the University of Arizona, one of my professors shared another interesting study Lorenz and his team had done with a group of ducks. Their pressing question: What if, right after baby ducks are born on the pond, the mommy duck not only is removed from the babies but is replaced by a basketball, complete with mother duck sounds and movement remotely controlled by the experimenters?

So, right after a group of baby ducks was born on the pond, the experimenters whisked Mama Duck away and replaced her with a remote-controlled basketball. What happened to those baby ducks? They bonded to the basketball. Anywhere that basketball floated, the baby ducks followed in a line.

What happened when the original Mama Duck was reinserted in that pond? The babies not only didn't follow her; they ignored her. They were too focused on that basketball because it had become "Mama."

In the critical period, the first 17 to 24 hours after a baby duck is born, that baby will bond with, and then follow, whatever moves. Hopefully, for the baby ducks, there will be a mother they can follow.

Why am I telling you about scientific experiments with birds? Because I'm convinced human beings, too, have that critical period. Just like recognizing "Mama" gives the geese youngsters a survival advantage, recognizing Mama teaches a baby about trust and love, gives security in a food source, and offers a warm introduction to the world.

Watch a mom with a young baby sometime. That infant actually does a dance in perfect sync with Mommy, listening to her voice, watching her movement, and responding accordingly. Everything Mama does—the softness with which she speaks, the way she laughs, the songs she sings at nighttime, even the sway of her body as she does that gentle movement only moms can do to lull the baby to sleep—creates an atmosphere of love and stability.

That child absorbs her mother's undivided attention like a sponge does water. And because she is so focused and bonded to Mommy, she will learn very quickly. She'll copy what Mom says and how she says it. She'll cock her head like Mom does and even put her hand on her hip. She'll mimic baking a pie with her playdough, using the same steps Mom takes to bake one. That's why, for example, if you want your child to flawlessly learn a second language, the optimal time to introduce it is from eighteen months to three years old. Even better if you speak it yourself and your child can watch and listen to you.

> Your children are your greatest fans.

Simply stated, your children are your greatest fans. What you role-model imprints permanently on them.

As Anne Ortlund once said, "Children are wet cement,"[3] moldable and impressionable. But as they grow older, that cement hardens, and it's more difficult to make impressions. That's why the best time to catch them is . . . as soon as you can.

But they can't watch you if you're not there, can they?

The Number One Thing You Can Do for Your Kids

Think back a few years, or many, depending on the ages of your kids. Do you remember the first time you looked into the eyes of your child? At that moment of imprinting?

I certainly do for each of my five children. With Holly, my 19.5-inch firstborn, I thought, *Wow, she's about the same size as the walleye pike I caught awhile back.*

A sense of responsibility, protectiveness, and, I admit, a bit of terror settled in. I didn't want my baby girl to be cold, so I cranked the heat up. By the time I brought Sande and baby Holly home from the hospital, the house was like an incubator at 104 degrees. My profusely sweating wife patiently said, "Honey, I gave birth to a child . . . not an African daisy."

I was a psychologist, but Sande and I still didn't have a clue what we were doing as first-time parents. We simply learned as we went along. Only one thing was certain in our minds: We were happy when our baby took a nap so we could clean ground zero and get ready for the next four hours. We were extra lucky if we could take a nap too.

As we parented Holly and then added four more—Krissy, Kevin II, Hannah, and Lauren—we did some things well, and our average increased as we added kids. But we also made mistakes. By the time Holly was an adolescent, I'd evidently made enough mistakes that she once declared vehemently at the dinner table, "You know what, Dad? You ought to read one of your own books!"

Ouch. Yet today, both of us are doing well, and our relationship has only grown closer over the years as we've weathered the changes together.

After surviving and thriving through parenting five children who are as different as day and night, I'm convinced that one of the most important things we did well was to pay attention to our kids.

Our decision to be *present* with our kids, from their earliest age forward, has everything to do with our healthy, ongoing relationships now that they are adults. Yes, it took some sacrifices, like having only one car for a number of years and creatively penny-pinching on housing, clothing, and meals, but the dividends are well worth it. No matter where our kids roam, they *want* to return home. They actually like their siblings and show up at each other's birthdays in other states. They text us and each other often. They make Leman family events a life priority even when they have extended families and expansive friend networks.

How do you get such kids who care about each other? It starts with your presence from the beginning, when that first munchkin shows up in your home. For some of you, that's the day you gave birth to your 20-incher. For others of you, it's the day you gained a stepdaughter or stepson. For still others, it's the day you adopted your six-month-old, five-year-old, or nine-year-old.

When our daughter Hannah adopted twin girls as babies, we learned even more about the importance of presence. Hannah was gifted with being present when those babies were born. Not all adoptive parents are that fortunate. But I know many other adoptive parents who, though they couldn't be there in their child's

---

HOW WE DO IT:

Jake and Rachel

My wife and I were entrenched in busy careers when we finally got the call we were waiting for from our adoption agency. Four-year-old Jessie joined our family a few months later.

Rachel had frequently traveled for her job but agreed with her company to cut her hours from her usual 45 or 50 to 30, and not to travel for at least the next several years. She also arranged to work only two days in the office during the week. On one of those days, my mom and dad, who live across town, get to spend time bonding with Jessie and attending a half-hour music class with her.

I swapped working on Fridays for Saturdays, so I have Fridays at home with Jessie while Rachel works. Sundays are Mommy, Daddy, and Jessie days—for the three of us.

We had to do a lot of juggling to make it all work, but the smile on my daughter's face is worth it.

early days, have gone out of their way to imprint on that child their love and care, and most of all, their time.

The concept of imprinting and the importance of a parental presence are why I encourage couples, whenever possible, to have one parent stay home with the kids. Or they can switch off staying at home—whether that means rearranging or reinventing work, cutting out expenses that aren't necessary for a higher priority, or asking other loved ones for additional assistance at home.

Just as it took two to tango to create that child or adopt that child, both partners need to be all in on the parenting journey. Those three weeks to four months of maternity leave automatically granted by a company you work for isn't enough time if you want to develop a close relationship with your child that will span your lifetime. Nobody can raise that kid like you, nor will anyone else be as invested in your child's long-term welfare.

If you're a single parent, staying home with your child may seem like a daunting, impossible task. But let me ask you: Aren't the possibilities worth investigating when your child's welfare is at stake? Could you work part-time? Do online work from home? Reinvent the type of work you do? Streamline expenses? Ask for help from trusted others? Swap a day of at-home care with another single mom? If two of you go to the same music class, could you switch off taking the children while one of you works?

If you don't try something, how do you know it wouldn't work? The options are as endless as your brainstorms. If you want some additional ideas, check out my book *Single Parenting That Works*.

How you accomplish that goal of spending as much time as possible in the home while your kids are growing up can be as unique as your situation. Flexibility is important. Some families streamline or downsize so Mom or Dad can step out of the workforce for a few years. Other moms move to part-time, with Grandma, a sister, or hubby being on point with baby the days or

HOW I DO IT:
Renee

I'm a single mom with a two-year-old. When my husband left soon after my son was born, I dusted off my skills as a music major and began teaching piano.

I teach from home four days a week during Callan's two-hour afternoon nap. On Friday my neighbor's high-school daughter baby-sits for three hours after school in exchange for a free weekly piano lesson on Saturday morning. They play together really well, especially at a time where Callan is showing signs of stranger anxiety.

On Saturdays, my brother and sister switch off picking up Callan during the day and take him to fun places like the park, the local butterfly farm, and the science museum for kids. I teach from 9:00 a.m. to 6:00 p.m., when Callan returns. The two hours after that are Mommy and Callan time.

Most Sundays we spend with my parents, who surround Callan with family love and send home dinner leftovers with us, which eases my Mondays. (I now call them "no cooking" days.) Sometimes my parents shoo me out the door to spend time with friends I wouldn't normally have time to see.

Every once in a while, my family helps out in a surprising way—like the time my car died and my brother and a mechanic friend fixed it for free. Or when my parents knew I'd had a rough month, and they gave me $300 toward my rent.

Pinching pennies isn't easy. It's not the life I would have chosen. But I'm grateful I found a creative way to spend time with the person who matters most to me: my son.

hours she's away from the home or needs to sleep. Some dads and moms start home businesses and work all kinds of crazy hours while their kids are sleeping. Their partners who may never have cooked or cleaned a day in their lives now come home from work and serve as cooks and housecleaners. I know one guy who, a few

HOW I DID IT:
Rebecca

I got married later in life to a wonderful dad of two teenage daughters, ages 13 and 15. They'd lost their mom when they were in elementary school. Before Rusty and I got engaged, I told the girls, "I know you loved your mom very much. I could never replace her. But will you allow me to be an older friend or aunt as we get to know each other?"

Those words were a first step in taking away potential fear or resentment. It didn't mean jealousy didn't crop up when they felt like I got too much of their dad's attention. Or that they didn't sometimes fire at me, "You're not my mom. Don't tell me what to do." But there were also small breakthroughs in their walls as they learned to love and accept someone new.

The morning of Andee's 16th birthday, I heard her crying in her room. I knocked lightly on the door. "Honey, can I come in?"

She was sitting on the bed holding a picture of her mother.

I sat beside her. "I know you miss your mom. And it's your birthday. I bet you wish she were here."

Andee sniffled and nodded.

I put my arm around her. "Well, if she were here, I bet she'd say how proud she is of you. That you're a smart, beautiful young woman who is gentle with her sister and loving toward other people. Just the other day I noticed . . ." And I told her the story of a sweet thing I'd seen her do for our next-door neighbor, who wasn't feeling well.

When she allowed me to hug her for a long time, it felt really good. I'd always wanted to be a mom. Even though I wasn't yet called one, she felt like my daughter.

Five years passed in a flash for Rusty and me. Our daughters are now both in college. (Note that I said "our.") And when they come home on break, guess what flies out of their mouth upon arrival?

"Mom, Dad, it's so good to see you!"

For anyone who's in the trenches of stepparenting, I have two pieces of advice: (1) Be loving and patient. (2) Hang in there. Good things come to those who wait. Those two girls calling me "Mom" is living proof.

years ago, couldn't even find the milk in the grocery store. Today he's a master online coupon shopper.

Never underestimate the value of your presence in the home. It imprints your love, care, and values onto your child. Even when he's a teenager whose behavior seems to say, "I don't want you in my life," trust me, he does. In fact, you're the person who keeps his tilted teen world from spinning off its axis into Neverland.

You only have a small window to make your mark, for the positive or the negative, on your child. Believe me, those 18 years when your child is in your home (or partly in your home, if you share custody with an ex) will fly by fast. When you're old like me, you won't say, "Oh, I wish I would have spent more time at work or on vacation." You'll say, "I wish I'd spent more time with my kids as they were growing up."

> Every child comes out of the womb craving attention. The question is, is he or she going to get it—from you?

Every child comes out of the womb craving attention. The question is, is he or she going to get it—from you? Even more, if *you* don't give your child attention, then who will? Nobody will care about your child the way you do. And no one can imprint on him or her the way you can. It takes time and your presence.

Don't abdicate your parental role to anyone—whether a counselor, a coach, a babysitter, a school principal, or a dance teacher. They might be the best in their field, but they're not you.

Only you will do.

Why You Do What You Do

How your background and experiences
influence your parenting more than you know.

Have you ever said, "I'm never going to say to my kids what my parents said to me"? But then you not only say those things but use the exact same words, only louder, with your own kids?

Welcome to the club. What goes around in your childhood usually comes around in your parenting unless you realize why you're doing and saying what you are and intentionally make changes. But why should you care about changing yourself when you bought this book because you're concerned about your child's behavior? Because any change in their behavior starts with a change in yours. As a wise coach I know once said, "They don't care what you know until they know that you care."

So in this chapter, we'll take a quick look back at your growing-up years. Everything that happened to you in your childhood is influencing your parenting now. That includes the parents you grew up with and how they treated you, the life mantra you created as a result of your experiences, and the way you interact with your kids.

Like Father, Like Son

I had a good laugh the other day as I was walking down a crowded city street. A father and his young son were waiting on the opposite side of a crosswalk at a red light. The father, Bluetooth device in one ear, was talking to an unknown person and gesturing with his hands. The son, smartphone in hand, eyed his father, yanked one of his earbuds out, and started gesturing too.

Any change in their behavior starts with a change in yours.

When the light turned green for the crosswalk, I met them in the middle of the street as the father said to his phone contact, "That's all for today." The young son looked up at his dad and then said seriously into his phone, "And that's all for today."

What was that young son doing? Mimicking his hero's actions.

All of us looked up to someone when we were kids. For me, it was my saintly mom who patiently endured all my antics, followed by my dad, my big brother, my big sister, and the local firemen who got to honk that really loud horn and run into buildings and save people like Superman.

When you were a kid, who did you look up to? Your mom? Your dad? An older sibling because your parents were MIA? Who was the one you wanted to be like when you grew up?

What was that person like? Encouraging? Fun loving? Confident? Easy to talk to? Respected by everybody? A bit bossy, but you could count on them to get the job done?

That person is the one who helped form your personality and life mantra the most. Following are four life mottos and the pros and cons of each. Which one sounds most like the hero you had as a child?

Let's Do It the Fun Way

Their life mantra: *I only count when I'm in the limelight—noticed, appreciated, and adored.*

Pros

The best description for Fun Ways is the *fun* that's in their name. They're spontaneous, the kind who jump into the water before researching how deep the pond is first. They put anything social, like arranging an extended-family barbecue, over unimportant things like cleaning out the garage or paying the electric bill. They don't bug you about studying for your upcoming AP science test because, frankly, they don't keep track of details and don't even remember you have the test. They're too busy thinking about their upcoming birthday party or the new iPad model they saw.

Fun Ways want to be noticed and appreciated for who they are and what they do. It's even better if you say things like, "Wow, you're the best parent ever," or "Nobody can make better kolacky than you. You could set up your own bakery."

Fun Ways laugh and smile a lot, can talk about anything to anyone, tell lively stories, and enjoy interacting with people in general. They're charming and have large social networks.

They also say things like, "Oh, you got an F on the test? Don't worry. You'll get an A next time." They're naively optimistic.

Cons

Fun Ways get discouraged easily when they're not in the limelight and can get resentful if you don't appreciate them. They're also disorganized, like the mom who forgot to pick up her second-grader at school because she was having too much fun socializing with a new friend she made at the grocery store.

Since they don't like to worry about things, they often let others do their work. Remember when your mom said she'd help you with that Kool-Aid stand when you were a kid, but she started chatting with another mom, walked off, and left you to do it all yourself?

Fun Ways always have their eye on the next fun prize, so they get bored easily and tend to jump from thing to thing. Remember the four home businesses your dad started when you were a kid? He was so happy for a few months, but then the hard work hit and he got discouraged fast. When anyone questioned his motives or criticized his actions, he deflated like a balloon with a pin stuck in him. "Why are you picking on me?" was his standard line, and then he'd leave to seek out someone he could have fun with.

When each of those businesses failed, he came up with lame excuses like, "Well, your mother didn't support me enough," or "I trusted Ted to make sure the finances were working, but he didn't handle that well."

His too-quick investments created a kink in the family income for years. You couldn't join the traveling soccer league you had your eye on, and your mom ended up working two part-time jobs to help make ends meet.

What You Learned from Your Fun Way Parent

If you had a positive growing-up experience with such a parent—where all was happiness, light, and laughter, and your family had plenty of money to weather the "If I see it and like it, I'll buy it" patterns of a Fun Way—then lucky for you. But be aware that most of the planet won't be able to relate to you. For the majority of people, life isn't a fairy-tale experience from start to finish.

If your Fun Way parent was your hero because he was always fun, someday you'll learn the hard way that being popular and adored and having fun aren't the only things or the most important things in life. And if you expect to have those kinds of experiences all the time, like you did as a child, well, you're going to be vastly disappointed with life in the real world.

> *For the majority of people, life isn't a fairy-tale experience from start to finish.*

It's more likely that you were on the receiving end of some trauma because of a Fun Way's disorganization, lack of follow-through on projects, and inability to budget money or their time. Perhaps your dad floated from job to job, which meant your family moved a lot. Or your mom embarrassed you by trying to act like your friend in public or by dressing goofy in front of your boyfriend or girlfriend.

As a result, you're going to be extra hard on your own child if she's disorganized, loses her pocket money, doesn't seem to take life seriously, and seems to major on socializing with others over studying. No way do you want her to turn out like a Fun Way.

Let's Do It My Way

Their life mantra: *I only count when I'm in charge and others immediately follow my orders.*

Pros

My Ways are impressive leaders. They're doers and hard workers who spend a lot of time doing their jobs. They have drive and energy and tend to do things themselves since they know they can do them better. They're at the head of the family pack for good reason—their confident, "big" presence. When they walk in the door at home, everybody pays attention.

When a My Way decides on a certain direction, he is never swayed to change his mind. You could predict what the My Way in your family would do. He was as firm as steel, commanding respect wherever he went, whether that was at work, at home, or in the community. Nobody messed with you because they didn't dare mess with him, since they knew they'd end up with the short end of the stick. He was in control of everything that happened in your family.

Cons

Because he was so self-confident, he made fast judgments. Once he'd decided, he wouldn't entertain new or different ideas. He said what he thought needed to be said, no matter if it hurt your feelings. Yes, usually he was right, but sometimes you wanted him to hear you out *before* he made up his mind or the parental hammer came down on you for doing something stupid.

He also didn't have a sympathetic bone in his body. He certainly never coddled you and rarely hugged you. You can't remember a single time in your entire growing-up years where he said, "I love you" or "I'm proud of you."

What You Learned from Your My Way Parent

On the good side, you never had to wonder what the road map at home was, because all the rules were set out in clear black-and-white. Mess with those rules and you were in trouble. The phrase "grounded for life" wouldn't be able to describe the rest of your existence at home. But adhere to the rules, be a good girl or boy, and you'd get along fine with the My Way. No, you wouldn't get a lot of hugs or affirmation, but every once in a while he'd give you a nod and a "good job."

On the flip side, you learned that if you had a problem, you better never reveal it. If you did, he'd swoop in and exact an almighty judgment that usually wasn't in your best interest or could mean social death for you as a teenager. So if you had a problem, you fixed it yourself . . . hopefully before he found out. You also learned that if he asked you to do something, you better stop everything and do it now, or you would pay.

> Mess with those rules and you were in trouble. The phrase "grounded for life" wouldn't be able to describe the rest of your existence at home.

He was a perfectionist, and you felt like you could never measure up to his standards. When you got a B in earth science, you got a stern lecture because you weren't working hard enough, even though you had As in everything else.

That critical-eyed parent of yours set you up to be your own worst enemy. No one has to put you down because you put yourself down: "I'm such a loser. I should have done a better job." You procrastinate starting a project because you know you'll never do a good enough job. Often you don't finish a project because it's better to be a slacker than a failure and a loser. You doubt yourself. *Am I good enough? Can I really do that, and do it the way it should be done? Should I even try?*

If you ever embarrassed your family in any way, you were in big trouble because it made your My Way dad look like a bad father. He never let you live it down. You were under his eagle eye from that point forward and labeled as a rebellious troublemaker, until your brother or sister did something to direct his eagle eye onto them. Nobody in your family dared question his pronouncements or his authority.

If you're a woman who grew up under a My Way dad and got married, chances are that you married somebody like good ol' Dad because you learned how to please someone like him and got comfortable with him calling the shots in your life. So when you started dating, you naturally found someone like him.

Now maybe you even have a My Way twofer to deal with: husband *and* firstborn son who act like your dad. If so, I wouldn't blame you for dreaming of a wee bit of revenge against dear old Dad and aiming it in the direction of your husband and son. You could never do anything well enough for your dad, and now you have two people critiquing you. All those things that your dad hated, like you questioning his judgment, dragging your feet in getting things done, dropping the ball on details, and hiding things from him, come in handy for driving the two other guys in your life bonkers.

If you're a man who grew up under a My Way dad, you're probably the apple that doesn't fall far from the tree. All those things your dad did to you? You'll do them to your kids, only magnified. You'll be the ultimate family controller. You'll make snap judgments, be impatience personified, run the family show, and not tolerate any questions from your kids. After all, you're the father, and they should do what you say, without any question, because you know what's best.

Problem is, because you're so dedicated to work, you don't really see your kids growing and changing or give them credit for what they're learning on their own. And without making intentional changes in your parenting, day by day you'll become the distant, unapproachable dad who mirrors your own father.

Let's Do It the Right Way

Their life mantra: *I only count when I can meet my own high standards by doing things right.*

Pros

Right Ways are organized, analytical, and good planners. They're thoughtful and sensitive of others' feelings. They live by high standards and ideals. They're idealistic and faithful to their families, having the best interests of the group in mind.

This person was a class act. So put together, in fact, that she was downright intimidating. Even on a Saturday morning, she'd be up, showered, and dressed in impeccably neat attire before the rest of you could even manage to extract yourself from bed. She loved to sit and drink coffee in a nook in your family room before the rest of the family was up. Quiet spaces were important to her. You never had to worry that she'd go off half-cocked and yell at you. If you had a new idea, she was the one you chose to discuss it with.

Right Ways are organized, analytical, and good planners.

When your father suddenly decided he wanted to move the whole family to North Carolina to form a company with a friend from college, she retreated for a day instead of telling him how crazy that idea was (though you kids vehemently did and got nowhere). When she did come up for air, she had a whole list of pros and cons regarding the move, many of which he'd never thought about.

Also, she was the one who broadened your horizons, the cultured one who made sure you attended a symphony concert and visited art galleries—something you'd once said you were interested in, even though you were on a sports team at the time. Outwardly you might have grumbled, but secretly you were glad for an excuse to give your teammates: "My mom is making me go."

Cons

She expected you to be as detailed, classy, and perfectionistic as she was, and none of those are your fortes. You felt like she was so perfect, you couldn't stack up to her.

Because she's such a long-range thinker, she was already discussing your future with you when you were a freshman in high school. When all you could think about was whether or not you could survive in the jungle of your first week of high school, discussing long-range plans like your choice of colleges and majors was stressful.

Sometimes you missed opportunities because it took her too long to think through them. Or, if she had a family dinner planned and you had an opportunity to do something unusual, like get free tickets to an event you could never afford, she'd say no. Sometimes you got tired of being on a schedule, even on the weekends. If you complained, you got the imperious brow lift and a mini lecture about how important it was to be disciplined.

There were also times you wished that she'd stand up for herself a little more when your dad had cockamamie ideas, but she was too respectful to speak up. Instead, you saw her retreat physically and get moody and negative. When she didn't like something, rather than argue, she'd give you the ice treatment and go away somewhere to be alone.

You had no clue she was insecure until she tried to get a part-time job but wasn't chosen. Then she hardly got out of bed for the next week.

Also, her friends were . . . well, boring. All they did was sit around and talk about ideas that didn't make any sense when you wanted them to play catch with you.

What You Learned from Your Right Way Parent

If you had to pick a great parent of the year, you'd pick this one and want to be like her—at least when she's at her best. She listened to you, was respectful of your ideas and time, kept things organized around the house so you could find your clothes and homework, and had your back. "Loyal" was her middle name.

When the neighbor accused you of squashing his hydrangeas, your mom brought him banana bread and said sweetly, "Your hydrangeas were lovely. I hate that they got squashed. But I did a bit of research. My son was at soccer practice from three to five o'clock when they got smashed. I did see a man walking a Great Dane in our neighborhood around that time. From the marks on your bushes, it's highly likely that dog is the culprit."

With those few details, your name was cleared, and there was peace between your house and the neighbor's again.

If your dad had confronted the neighbor, it would have been like World War III on the block.

Now, if your dad had confronted the neighbor, it would have been like World War III on the block. In contrast, your mom never embarrassed you in public. Nor did she invade your room like your sister did, because she was big on privacy herself.

Because of those qualities you admired about her, you also respect your kids' privacy, even when they don't want to talk. You have their back and help them organize their homework and activities. You try to introduce ethnic foods and information about other cultures and news from around the world, even if doing so gets a few groans of "Not again . . ."

But you also expect your kids to meet the same high standards your mom expected you to meet. If they don't get all As, you push them to do better. If they aren't as organized or detail oriented as you, you give them friendly "suggestions."

If you sense they aren't telling you the truth about an event, you're suspicious and check out the facts behind the scenes. When they catch you at it, the inevitable "You don't trust me" is flung your way. Because you don't deal well with confrontation, you tend to exit as soon as your kids are upset, so the matter doesn't get fully resolved.

You're hardest on your youngest child, who seems to charm and entertain others with his clown-like qualities but annoys you to your core. You tend to hate groups, which is something he thrives on, so you don't understand his bent to put social activities first. When he bypasses time with you to spend time with friends, you resent that and tend to hold a grudge against him.

You're more comfortable with your predictable oldest child, who is more of a loner like you and has high standards himself. But since you're a perfectionist who is specific about what you want and how you want it, you always find room for improvement even in that child. Your critical eye causes a great deal of friction between you. You can't stand when things aren't done correctly— the right way and in the right order. But neither can your firstborn, so sometimes the two of you are like rubbing sandpaper with the resulting sparks.

Let's Do It the Easy Way

Their life mantra: *I only count when everybody likes me and I can keep the peace.*

Pros

This parent was a great companion, ever present when you wanted to talk. When you got home late from an event, he was sitting in the living room waiting for you. He was patient, loyal, and balanced in his assessments, willing to hear your side of the story. He was also tolerant of your antics, with a shrug and the words "I guess every kid tries that sometime."

If you could use one word to describe an Easy Way, it would be *peacemaker*. He never got upset with anyone. Everyone liked him because he was helpful and could adapt to any situation. He was an incredible

If you could use one word to describe an Easy Way, it would be peacemaker.

listener, so even the crotchety grandpa in the apartment next door loved him.

When tough things happened, he would nod and say, "That's to be expected. Things can't always be easy. Everybody has some rough times in life. We'll get through it."

When you wanted someone to stick by your side in getting a boring project done, like painting the house during spring break, the Easy Way was your ready partner. He didn't quit until it was done and didn't seem to mind the more-than-average breaks you took.

Cons

"Bland" was his middle name. As you overheard your grandma say once, "Well, he'll never set the world on fire." That's an understatement. An Easy Way is never quick acting and impulsive. He wants everyone to like him, so he works hard to keep the peace and sidestep conflict, even if that means he gets the bad end of the stick.

Like the time he took the blame for something a coworker did and got demoted at work. That was annoying enough because you hated that he couldn't stand up for himself. But when he backed off from what was truly important to you because he didn't want to make waves, that hurt deeply. You started to see him as someone who couldn't make a decision one way or another because he didn't want to disappoint anyone. That often left the people he loved in no-man's-land, stuck in the middle between two options. Just once you wanted to see him fight for something he cared about instead of agreeing with what others wanted.

As you became a teenager, he was popular with your friends since he was amiable and kind. He helped them with anything, even if that meant he didn't get done what he'd promised you. Because he switched gears to please people on the spot, his actions seemed aimless. And since he took the time to listen to people rather than finish a project, he often appeared lazy.

What You Learned from Your Easy Way Parent

When you wanted someone to hear what you were thinking and back you up in presenting an event to your other parent, who wouldn't welcome it, your Easy Way parent was the one you went to. He was so pliable that you often played him against your mom, to be truthful. You could also get him to do your projects if you didn't want to do them.

But his lack of energy and his inability to make decisions because he was afraid of disappointing people really grated on you. You wanted to yell, "Would you tell me what you honestly think instead of dancing around the subject?" Or, "Why can't you stand up for yourself?"

Also, his indecisiveness and his ability to change with whatever wind was blowing in the house ended up putting you in a tough situation more than once. Yes, he had your back . . . but only if your mom wasn't upset about it. If she was, your dad would placate her as much as he could, then rest in his easy chair until the temperature in the house had cooled to normal.

With your own kids, you try to mirror your Easy Way parent's best qualities: being patient, tolerant, and understanding of your kids' misbehavior. Remembering the times that your dad didn't have your back, though, can make you fiercely protective of your kids to outsiders, even if your kids are in the wrong.

You are toughest on the kid who seems to go with the flow the most. Because you wish you'd known what your Easy Way parent thought, you prod your child with pointed questions, such as:

- "So what do you think?"
- "Why aren't you annoyed? This situation would bother me, but you seem so calm."
- "Don't you think you're letting that person take advantage of you because he knows you'll never fight?"

- "Why don't you stand up for yourself? Are you really going to take that?"
- "I know your friend was having a tough time, but did you have to spend three hours listening to him? What about your history paper due tomorrow?"

Those questions are a retro stab at the Easy Way parent you had. To your kid, though, they'll seem like stabs out of the blue, and he'll wonder, *What's wrong with Dad?*

It's Your Turn

Take a few minutes to think about your parent(s) or the guardian you grew up with (perhaps an older brother or aunt). Though people can often be a mixture of types, which type was that person most like?

- The Fun Way wants to have fun.
- The My Way wants to get things done.
- The Right Way thinks about *how* something should be done so it gets done correctly.
- The Easy Way patiently works the angles so no one's feathers will be ruffled.

Can you see how the pros and cons of those types affected who you've become as a parent? And how those types resulted in the life mantra you formed of "I only count when . . ."?

So which one below sounds most like you?

Fun Way: I only count when . . .

- I'm in the limelight and others notice me.
- I'm appreciated and applauded.

- I can make people laugh.
- People think I'm adorable.
- My schedule is full and busy with social activities.
- I'm popular.
- Everybody accepts me and thinks I'm wonderful.
- People are interested in me.

My Way: I only count when . . .

- I'm top dog.
- Others respect me.
- I'm successful.
- I'm in control.
- I'm appreciated for my accomplishments.
- I get things done.
- Others obey me immediately.

Right Way: I only count when . . .

- I get things done correctly.
- I can think through projects thoroughly before I do them.
- I meet my own high standards.
- I effectively set long-range goals and follow them.
- I'm organized.
- Other people appreciate—and follow—my detailed, well-thought-out plan.

Easy Way: I only count when . . .

- Everybody around me is happy and gets along.
- I can keep the peace.
- I can please others.

- I don't rock the boat.
- I avoid conflict.
- Others like me.

Got your answer?

If your life mantra is "I only count when people like me and think I'm wonderful" (Fun Way), how are you going to deal with your kids' misbehavior? You'll probably avoid the situation by not dealing with it. You'll exit the premises and go out for an evening with the friends who think you're wonderful. Those kids may get off scot-free momentarily, but their unchecked behavior will grow worse until you are forced to deal with it . . . perhaps by someone outside your family who isn't enamored with your "fun" ways.

If your life mantra is "I only count when I'm top dog and others respect me" (My Way), how will you deal with your kids' misbehavior? You'll come down like an almighty hammer to judge your kids before they can open their mouths to explain any behavior. You might get immediate outward obedience because those kids view you as top dog. But trust me, resentment is simmering under the surface. The next time they misbehave, they'll be sneakier about it so they don't get caught.

If your life mantra is "I only count when projects meet my high standards because they get done correctly" (Right Way), then you're really in trouble. This time those "projects" are your kids, and it will be impossible for them to meet your high standards and do life correctly even on their best days. Kids aren't projects; they're people, and they have their own minds. Just because you think they should act a certain way doesn't mean *voilà*—they will do that. Your natural disposition to become discouraged and resentful won't help resolve the misbehavior. It will only further alienate you from your kids.

If your life mantra is "I only count when everybody likes me, gets along, and is happy" (Easy Way), oh boy, are you in trouble.

Sure, you can try to hide your misbehaving kid's antics from your partner by trying to fix things on the side, but that won't last long. By rescuing your child from the consequences of his behavior, you're hurting him long-term. That same kid who put dish detergent in the fish bowl in first grade becomes the sixth-grade researcher who mixes a mini bomb to put in the teacher's trash can. If you don't pay attention to that kid now instead of trying to keep the peace, a situation will come along that will force you to address it.

Just because you think they should act a certain way doesn't mean voilà— they will do that.

So, let me ask you: When do you count?

As you consider your own life mantra, formed as a result of your interactions with your parent(s) and growing-up experiences, what have you learned about how you view and react to your child's misbehavior? For your child's behavior to change, you have to be aware of and adjust your "I only count when" perspective.

Remember, "They don't care what you know until they know that you care." But when they know, the progress you can make will amaze you.

As Dr. Seuss said, "Oh, the places you'll go" . . . together.

Programming Misbehavior

---

*How you unwittingly pave the way
for your child to misbehave.*

It was 10:05 p.m., and I was winding down from a long day when my eighth-grade son, Kevin II, approached me with a handful of papers.

"Dad, would you help me with these spelling words?" he asked.

"No," I said, reaching for the TV remote control.

"Dad! I have a big test tomorrow," he added, brandishing the papers in my direction.

"The answer is no," I restated in an even tone.

"If I flunk that test, it's gonna be your fault," my son said.

"Think for a minute about what you're saying," I replied. "But still, I'm not helping." Back I went to my channel surfing.

He stomped off to his room and slammed the door. I heard a few items being kicked across the floor. It was quite a dramatic show, rivaling anything on TV at the moment.

Right now some of you reading this are shocked. *What a terrible dad*, you're thinking. *Is a TV brain rinse more important than your kid? You should have helped him to do well, especially since he asked. What's wrong with you?*

Here's what's wrong. On that night when he should have been studying for the spelling test and should have asked for my help earlier if he needed it, my son, who loves magic, watched the David Copperfield special on television from 8:00 to 10:00.

Context sure helps when faced with your kid's misbehavior, doesn't it?

When Kevin II continued to stomp around and make a big fuss in his room, my blood pressure started to rise, and I had thoughts of retribution. I'm only human.

So I did the smart thing. I waited a bit until I was in control of my emotions and he'd also cooled down. Then I knocked on his door. "May I come in?"

"Sure," my son said in a suddenly happy tone.

I knew what that meant. He thought I'd changed my mind.

> Context sure helps when faced with your kid's misbehavior, doesn't it?

I entered and sat on his bed. "Hey, Kevin, from eight to ten this evening you were watching TV. Then you come to me at five minutes after ten, past what you know is my bedtime, with this hard-luck story. It seems to me that if you really cared about your spelling words, you would have been on them earlier."

He made a last desperate try. "Well, you gonna help me?"

I shook my head. "I already made that clear. But I do want to be the first to wish you good luck on the test."

Then I exited the bedroom.

The next morning Kevin II was up very early in the kitchen studying spelling on his own.

Now, you tell me: Would he have been studying on his own if I had rescued him the night before? If I would have said, "Poor boy, I know spelling is hard for you. How can I help?"

Nope.

Instead, would we have replayed this scene many more times, with him doing what he wanted to do first (watching a TV show) before he carried out his responsibility (taking care of his schoolwork)?

Yep. Isn't the definition of insanity doing the same thing over and over and expecting a different result?

Or how about if I'd said, "You know better than to bother me now with your work. It's *your work*, so get going. I work hard for this family, and I'm already done for the day. You should have done it earlier"?

All that rebuttal would have done was fuel the fire already burning in my son.

After that experience, my son paid a lot more attention to his homework earlier in the evening. He knew Dad wouldn't back down. He did try to hit on Mom's sympathy a time or two. Then again, Sande is married to a psychologist, so she didn't let him get away with it either.

Did my refusal to help damage his "psyche," as some of you worry about? Far from it. Today Kevin II is known across his industry as a very responsible hard worker who finds creative ways to not only get the job done but get it done well. Funny thing is, he's now the executive producer and head writer of two of the most watched television programs today. All those shows he loved to watch were good background preparation. Who would have known?

How You Create the Situation

At the end of chapter two, I made this statement: "Every child comes out of the womb craving attention. The question is, is he or she going to get it—from you?" Now I'd like to add these words: "Is he or she going to get it positively or negatively?"

If your kids can't get your attention through positive behavior, they'll proceed to get it with misbehavior, which they'll continue until you have to pay attention. That's why you, parent, have unwittingly paved the way for your child's misbehavior. You've done a great job, too, from the looks of it, so pat yourself on the back.

> *Don't start habits with kids that you don't want to continue through their college years.*

Here's one of the cardinal rules of parenting: Don't start habits with kids that you don't want to continue through their college years. Kids are creatures of habit. Any learned behavior will be repeated.

Yet take a look at the things we do:

"Look at the airplane. Zoom . . . it's getting closer. You have to open the hangar for the plane to land."

"Try it. You'll like it."

"Eat it. There are lots of starving kids in Africa who would love to have what you have."

"Oooh, look at that comfy bed. Which of your animal friends would you like to sleep with you tonight?"

"If you don't go to bed, the sleep fairies can't come visit you."

"I told you to stay in bed, so stay in bed."

"I don't care if you're 15. Your bedtime is 10:00 p.m. Lights out."

"It's time to sit on the potty. Just try. I'll give you a treat if you do."

"See all those special little cups? They're magic cups. If you drink them, you'll have special powers."

"Oh, look at the poo-poo. Honey, come quick. He went potty all by himself!"

"If you don't go potty, you can't go to preschool tomorrow."

"You're going to be the only kid in high school wearing diapers. You want that?"

Can you really *make* a child mind? No, but you can give her impetus to mind.

Can you really *make* a child eat? No, but he can sit with you at the table with his plate in front of him like the rest of the family. If he doesn't eat, the refrigerator, pantry, and freezer are closed until the next meal. No sneaking him snacks because you feel bad. He simply misses his meal. His growling stomach will do the trick of reminding him he's hungry and needs to eat.

Can you really *make* a child go to sleep? No, but you can insist she go to her room and stay there when it's bedtime. The natural process of sleep will happen sooner or later.

Can you really *make* a child go potty or potty train? No, he has to have the urge for that himself. Maybe he sees big brother or big sister go potty. Or he wants to go to preschool like big brother, but you tell him he has to be potty trained first. And does anyone give you special drinks and treats when you go potty? Then why should you do that for your child?

Eating, sleeping, and going potty are all natural things. Yet from the get-go we parents create habits around those things that prompt the beginning of misbehavior. Those misbehaviors grow as your kids have more encounters with you.

Once your kids have your number, you're done for . . . especially if you don't know what they're really thinking and scheming. What's prompting their misbehavior? Let's take a look at a few scenarios.

Scenario #1

Your nine-year-old wants to be in Little League this summer. You're all for it, but your husband isn't. Your kid pitches a fit and refuses to eat dinner.

What your nine-year-old is thinking:

Oh, I get it. Mom and Dad aren't on the same page here. If I try to get what I want from Dad, he'll come at me like a fast pitch. But you know, that's going to be in my favor. I'll let him do that. In fact, I'll fuel it a bit by being over the top myself.

I know exactly what Mom will do. She'll come running in and say, "John, you're being entirely too rough with Bradley lately."

They'll talk, and she'll pave the way. It won't be a problem to play Little League.

I got this.

Scenario #2

Your 14-year-old and 16-year-old have a 10:30 bedtime but don't want to go to bed. They want to watch a movie, so they scheme together.

Kid 1: "Okay, so Mom and Dad go to bed at 11:00. All we need to do is stall a little until they're too tired to say no."

Kid 2: "Oh, I got it. I'll tell Mom I have a big test tomorrow and beg her to let me study a bit more so I can feel more prepared. She can't say no to that."

Kid 1: "Great idea. You learned something from me, huh?"

Kid 2 grins. "Yeah. So what are you gonna do?"

Kid 1: "I'll stall Dad by telling him I've been thinking about my future. He loves that stuff. I'll get him going talking about college. You know how he is. He could talk about his days at Stanford forever. He won't even know what hit him until his bedtime. When I ask about watching the movie, he'll do that little hand wave and say, 'Sure, enjoy yourself.'"

Kid 2: "But what if we can't stall them long enough?"

Kid 1: "That's easy. We wake up Jemmie. She'll throw a fit, and Mom and Dad will come running. They'll be so distracted, they won't pay any attention to us."

Scenario #3

Your 12-year-old hates to do his chores, especially taking out the garbage. He conveniently forgets, stalls for time, or complains about doing it.

What your 12-year-old is thinking:

There it is again. Why do I get all the nasty jobs?

Hmm, how can I get out of it this time? Complaining about it doesn't get me anywhere. I just get "the look" and then, "Get to it."

Last time I faked stomach cramps and then had to exit the bathroom and go straight to school. Mom didn't want me to be late.

This time, let's see . . . Oh, I know. I'll help my little brother get dressed for school since he can't tie his shoes yet. Mom wants me to be nicer to him and bond and stuff.

Yeah, that'll work.

Scenario #4

Your 16-year-old daughter has had a bad day at school. She got stabbed in the back by her best friend, and then a teacher gave her grief for her handwriting on a test. She wants to take it out on someone, but if she acts up at school, she'll get a reputation she doesn't want. She's got to fight with someone to let off steam, so she takes it out on you the instant she walks in the door.

What your 16-year-old is thinking:

All I have to do when I walk in the door is give Mom an eye roll. That'll get things started fast. She hates that.

"What's wrong with you?" she'll say.

"Nothing."

She hates when I say that even more.

"Then keep your 'nothing' to yourself and come out when you don't have an attitude," she'll say.

"I had a really crappy day," I'll say, "and I don't need you lecturing me."

That'll escalate the fight for sure. And I'll feel a whole lot better after letting someone have it.

Mom'll take it. She always does.

This, parent, is what your child is really thinking and how well they can read a situation. They know exactly what to say or do to escalate a situation to get exactly what they want. They also know when not to say or do something to smooth things over before the hammer descends. If you have more than one kid, the enemy will unite for a frontal attack.

How do we usually respond to these kinds of situations? In one of two ways. Let's take a look at them.

The Two Most Common Types of Parenting

Most of us have learned how to parent by watching our parents. If you were raised in the typical home, you experienced one of two extreme parenting styles. Either you were expected to obey without question because you were the child and he was the parent, or you called the shots and she smoothed your road in life.

Note that I used "he" with the first style and "she" with the second style. I'll explain why in a minute. First, let's look at each of the parenting styles.

Parenting style #1: "It's my way or the highway."

Do any of these phrases sound familiar?

- "Look at me when I'm talking to you."
- "You better straighten up, or else."
- "I'm in charge, and I decide . . ."
- "How dare you question me. I'm your father."
- "If you don't like it here, you can leave."
- "You know what I expect, and this isn't it."
- "You better do what I tell you to do."
- "You're only a kid. What would you know?"
- "I've never met someone so stupid. And you had to be my son."

If one of your parents controlled your home with an iron fist, nine times out of ten it was your father. His expectation was iron-clad: "Do what I say, when I say it . . . or else." The threat was unspoken, but you felt it in every muscle fiber. It was in your best interest to jump to do whatever he expected you to.

This kind of parent is *authoritarian*. He used reward and punishment to control you. Usually the reward was fairly slim and didn't happen that often. But the punishment was harsh, swift, and predictable, like clockwork. Do one tiny thing wrong or not fast enough and you'd get hammered. Embarrass him in any way and you would be finished.

> *Do one tiny thing wrong or not fast enough and you'd get hammered. Embarrass him in any way and you would be finished.*

Because you were a child and he was older and bigger, he saw himself as better than you. But that's not true. Parents aren't better than their children. We're all equal in almighty God's eyes. We simply play different roles and have different responsibilities.

Authoritarian parents have a "you better do what I tell you to do, and fast" mind-set. This style worked in the short term, when they could physically control you and make you go to your room. But as soon as you entered your adolescent years, you had your own thoughts about what you wanted to do. All you had to do was fly under the radar of the authoritarian, and you could get away with it. You learned how to be sneaky.

By the time you entered high school, you had inward rebellion down pat.

Or maybe, when you had your own wheels, you threw any caution to the wind. What could he do to you now, when you could get away before he got home and stay overnight at a friend's? All you had to do was make it through graduation, and then you could move out. Then no one could tell you what to do again. You counted the days, or years, until you'd be free.

Parenting style #2: "I only want you to be happy."

Do any of these phrases sound familiar?

- "When you're happy, I'm happy."
- "Any way I can help you, I'm more than willing to do it."
- "Don't worry about that. I'll take care of it."
- "You're the best child ever."
- "That teacher doesn't seem to like you? I'll have to speak to him about that."
- "I can't believe someone did that to you. How dare they."
- "What do you want to do? I'll do whatever you want."
- "Oh, that paper is due tomorrow? I'll get right on it."
- "Your BFF doesn't like you anymore? Don't worry. You'll find a new one. I'll help you."

If these words came out of one of your parents' mouths, it was likely your mother's. That's because there are more women who are pleasers, while more men are controllers. As I said on CBN once, "There are nine pleaser males in the continental United States. However, we're not releasing their names or addresses!"[4]

Parents who just want their kids to be happy are *permissive*. They would sacrifice anything for their children, and they act more like servants than parents. If your mom was like this, you were brought up with what I call the "Disneyland Experience." You were the center of your family's universe. Anything you wanted, she tried hard to get for you. Anything you wanted to do, she pulled strings to arrange it. People saw you as a little princess, and you might have acted a bit like it too. Or they called you a mama's boy behind your back.

> You were the center of your family's universe. Anything you wanted, she tried hard to get for you. Anything you wanted to do, she pulled strings to arrange it.

Problem is, when you had to start making decisions for yourself, you weren't quite sure how to do it. The choices in front of you were paralyzing. You didn't have any experience in making decisions, because your parent did that for you. She didn't want you to be worried, bothered, or stressed, so she handled any situation that arose. But now you *are* all of those things because she robbed you of learning experiences. You find it difficult to make choices, or you make not-so-good ones and are shocked by the fallout. After all, Mama rescued you for years, no matter what. But in your adult life, you've discovered there are some things even Mama can't rescue you from.

Though you thought your mom was being nice or was a pushover, the reality is that she was as controlling as your dad—only in the opposite direction.

Why Both Parenting Styles Provoke Misbehavior

Authoritarian and permissive parents may seem poles apart, but they use a similar technique. Both make decisions *for* their children instead of teaching them how to make wise, informed choices for themselves. One parent does it with a stout club, and the other does it with the stroke of a feather, but the result is the same. Both extremes rob kids of the self-respect gained by making age-appropriate choices and learning from their mistakes.

> *Both extremes rob kids of the self-respect gained by making age-appropriate choices and learning from their mistakes.*

Authoritarian and permissive parenting styles also provoke misbehavior. Look at it this way. Did *you* like it when your parents made decisions for you? No. You may have had thoughts like these:

- I'm not that dumb. Who does he think I am, anyway?
- It'd be nice if they trusted me, just once.
- Do they really think I can't figure that out for myself?
- Give me a break. I'm 13. And she thinks I can't pick out my own jeans?
- Who does he think he is . . . God?
- Why did she have to talk to my teacher? It's so embarrassing. I could have handled it myself.
- Why can't he listen to my side of the story?
- I'm not a baby anymore, but she treats me like one.

If you didn't dare show your dad what you really thought, you certainly acted it out in your mind. When you could rebel outwardly and escape his reach, you did.

When your mom made too many decisions for you, you also rebelled by treating her like a slave in her own home. After all, she did your bidding, right? Even behind your father's back sometimes? Because she smoothed your roads in life, you lost respect for her.

Now, let me ask you something: Which of the two parenting styles do you lean more toward in your own parenting? "My way or the highway" or "I only want you to be happy"?

If both spouses are united on this parenting journey, it's highly likely that there is one parent of each type in the home. That's because opposites attract, and controllers are often attracted to "I only want you to be happy" pleasers, and vice versa.

This is especially true if a boy grows up in a home with a pleaser mama, and a girl grows up in a home with a controller father. For the boy, that version of a female is the one he's most comfortable with and pursues. Ditto for the girl and her father. She may have resentment toward her controller father, but she'll pursue someone similar to him because she knows how to act with him to get the desired responses. That's why the cycle continues. For both, it's like wearing the aged slippers they're used to and settling into that worn easy chair. *Ah* . . .

But there's a better way for you and your kids—a parenting style that can stay consistent even in the face of your child's hurricane winds. It doesn't raise your blood pressure. And it works every time.

The Only Way to Rear a Child

*Why being in healthy authority over
your kid is the best way to fly.*

One evening after I spoke in a big city, a frazzled-looking mom approached me. "Dr. Leman, I've read several of your books, including *Making Children Mind without Losing Yours* and *The Birth Order Book*. I really like them, but . . ." She looked down. "They don't work for me, because I'm a carpool mom."

I was about to ask, "And what parent isn't these days?" but she rushed on.

"My 10-year-old has a hard time getting out of bed. When I finally manage to get him up, my older kids are standing at the door, angry because they have to wait for him to get ready. By the time we pick up the other kids in the carpool, all of the kids are late to school. My kids are mad at me and embarrassed. The other kids are upset. And the other moms give me a piece of their minds when their kids tell them what happened.

"This is the third week it's happened, and I'm worried about getting kicked out of the carpool. I have to work three days a week, so there's no way I could take the kids to school every day."

"Getting kicked out of the carpool is the least of your worries," I said. "The most important is addressing your son's misbehavior."

"Misbehavior?" She raised an eyebrow. "He's just tired in the morning. He's having a hard time adjusting to the school schedule."

"He's ten. He knows the ropes of school by now. Would you ever be willing to leave him home and take the other kids to school?"

"Oh, I couldn't do that," she said.

That boy was workin' his mama because he could. And that permissive mama was allowing him to pull her chain and control the entire household from his bed. So I gave her some advice based on a third parenting style: *authoritative parenting.*

> *Sometimes you need to pull the rug out and let your misbehaving kid tumble if you want things to change.*

"Sometimes you need to pull the rug out and let your misbehaving kid tumble if you want things to change," I said. "In this case, words won't accomplish a thing. It's time for action."

I proposed that she leave the 10-year-old sleeper behind on the next school morning and take the other kids to school on time. That mom was finally desperate enough to do that after the other carpool moms gave her an ultimatum: Get the kids to school on time or be ousted from the carpool.

Later she reported back to me what had happened when she followed my advice.

Here comes the funniest part. When she pulled up to her house after running the other kids to school, guess where that 10-year-old was standing? The one who has never been concerned about time in his entire life? Right at the outside edge of their carport.

When she opened the car door, he flew at her. "Mom, do you know what time it is?"

She looked at her watch. "Yes, it's about ten after nine."

"I'm supposed to be at school at 8:30," he spouted.

"Oh, honey, would you like a ride to school?" she asked sweetly. "I'd be happy to give you a ride."

Her son, already dressed and wearing his backpack, jumped into the car. Still mad as a hornet, he continued trying to pick a fight with her.

She didn't say, "I told you that if you weren't ready, this would happen." That's because a parent who is in healthy authority over their kid doesn't threaten, "If you don't do this, I'm going to do that."

Even though he tried to fight with her all the way to school, she kept a happy face. When he exited the car, she even said, "Have a great day," and smiled.

What happened to him next wasn't quite so happy. He slammed the door and stomped into his classroom, and within 10 minutes there was an announcement over the loudspeaker.

A parent who is in healthy authority over their kid doesn't threaten, "If you don't do this, I'm going to do that."

"Timothy Adams, please report to the office. Timothy Adams . . ."

What do they want with me? he thought, panicked, on the walk to the assistant principal's office.

There was a long line of people waiting, so he had even longer to worry. At last the assistant principal ushered him into his office.

"Timothy, what time does school start?"

The kid straightened up into soldier posture. "Oh, 8:30, sir."

"What time were you here?" the assistant drill sergeant asked.

Soldier: "Uh, 9:45."

Assistant drill sergeant: "What time are you going to be here tomorrow?"

Soldier: "8:30, sir."

End of problem.

You see, what that boy didn't know is that I'd also encouraged his mom to do something else to resolve the issue: "After you drop that kid off at his regular door, park and go visit the school office. Talk to them and tell them what you're trying to achieve. Enlist their support. They'll be more than happy to oblige. They don't want a kid who's late all the time either."

You see, sometimes you have to work hard to dig out the consequence that will leave an impact on your child's mind and change his behavior. You've already tried multiple parenting strategies, including being authoritarian and permissive, as well as tips you've gained online or from other books. You know none of them work.

It's time to try something that does.

Parenting That Works

For you to be in healthy authority over your child, you need to be the advocate who role-models responsibility and good decision making. Every person is responsible for his or her own choices and actions. When your child fails—and he will—the world doesn't end for you or for him. Instead, the child walks away from his misbehavior with a life lesson he won't easily forget.

This kind of parenting style is called *authoritative*.

An authoritative parent doesn't command or preach. When his kid makes a mistake, he doesn't say, "You're such an idiot. If a bird had your brain, it would fly sideways." When his kid misbehaves, he doesn't layer on grounding until she's a teenager. He knows that he, too, is a fallible human being. We all make mistakes, have bad days, and feel cranky or mean from time to time.

When her child is upset, an authoritative parent doesn't try to fix what happened. When her child is struggling, she doesn't pave the way. Instead, she listens, lets her child brainstorm solutions and solve her own problem, and watches from the sidelines.

If you're an authoritative parent, you look for what I call "teachable moments." Instead of rescuing your kid from the consequences of his misbehavior, you let reality do the teaching:

- You establish boundaries to keep your child safe.
- You allow her to make age-appropriate decisions so she learns how to make decisions.
- You allow him to experience real-life consequences instead of living in a falsely constructed dream world.
- You provide opportunities for her to become responsible.
- You listen to him and support him but never do for him what he should do for himself.
- You allow her to make wrong decisions and experience the results of misbehavior within the loving boundaries of your home.

Believe me, a child knows when he's made a mistake. He doesn't need his nose rubbed in it. He also knows when he's misbehaving and getting away with it. With all that misbehavior, he's crying for attention. He wants you to care enough to stop him, but he doesn't know how to tell you that.

The way you handle things and your attitude have everything to do with whether your child stops that misbehavior or accelerates it. They also have everything to do with whether your child takes all that extra energy he's dedicated to misbehaving and turns it in a positive-attention direction.

Want Your Kids to Talk to You? Try This.

If you want your kids to talk to you, don't ask them questions.

Kids and husbands have a lot in common—both hate questions. Husbands don't have the nerve to tell their wives how much they detest the *why* word. Kids? Boys will grunt a nonsensical response, girls will flash a dramatic eye roll, and both will focus back on their iPhones within three seconds.

"But Dr. Leman, I think it's very important to ask my child how his day was when he gets home from school," you say.

Okay, let's replay that usual dog and pony show.

You: "How was your day?"

Son: "Fine."

You: "What did you do?"

Son: "Nothin'."

End of conversation.

Wasn't that stimulating? You're frustrated, and he's now in his room texting his buddies like a woodpecker with a bad case of ADHD. The slamming door was his signal of systematically shutting you out of his life.

Why? Think about it. Do *you* want to be asked questions right when you come home from work or from a night out with friends? Neither does he.

"If I don't ask questions, I'll *never* find out anything that's going on in my kid's life," you say.

That flat out isn't true. Kids—even alien creatures like adolescents—actually want to feel included and understood by their family. They crave unconditional love. They desire to be valued, respected, and taken seriously. Attempting to extract information through interrogation isn't respectful. Saying things like, "We need to talk" is an ironclad technique to guarantee a clamped-shut mouth (again, similar to husbands). Parental lectures and reminders fall on deaf ears because kids become parent-deaf.

So how do you get your kids to talk? Try these three winning strategies.

Offer short statements.

Your 13-year-old looks teary-eyed after school. Your Mama Bear instinct rises. *Who would dare hurt my little cub?* You force your reaction down and instead say quietly, "I can tell you had a rough day. If and when you want to talk about it, I'm all ears."

You don't press or pursue her when she drops her backpack in a heap on the kitchen floor and goes off to her room by herself. You've invited her to share *when she's ready*, and now you wait. Believe me, when she isn't forced, she *will* share . . . on her own timetable. When she does, you'll learn far more about her, her world, and her stresses than you've ever dreamed.

Say, "Tell me more about that."

Kids can be illogical, creative, and as dumb as mud. But when they throw you a curveball, you don't have to *react* with your emotions. You can choose to *respond*. The simple phrase "Tell me more about that" is a great door opener.

Your nine-year-old announces, "I want to go live with Daddy." That's impossible because your ex now lives in South America, and there's a lot you could spout about that idea. Instead, you say, "I bet you miss your daddy. Tell me more about that." You find out "Take Your Dad to School Day" is next week, and your son didn't want to tell you because he knew you'd feel bad.

Your 15-year-old declares at dinner that she's going to a pop concert in a different state. You swallow the mashed potatoes with the "What on earth are you thinking?" harangue that immediately pops into your head. Instead, you say, "You must really like that group. Do you have a song of theirs on your iTunes playlist that I could listen to sometime?"

You learn not only about her current music tastes but also about her friends, the peer pressure she's under, and a whole lot more in the next 24 hours, before her BFF decides they're no longer BFFs and the event is off.

Solicit their opinions.

Asking for an opinion is different from asking questions. Everyone loves to share their opinion. However, most families have that alpha firstborn who excels in nearly every area and dominates the sibling group. Telling the child who grows up in the shadow of his older sibling, "I'd love to know what you think," is like winning the lottery for him.

So pull aside that child and say, "May I ask your opinion on something?"
"Sure, Dad, what?"
"Is it me, or is your sister a little over the top?"

Wow, someone knows how I feel and what I'm up against every day, your overshadowed child thinks. Suddenly the 14-year-old who's usually as mute as an Egyptian sphinx is talking nonstop.

Everyone wants to feel valued, to be respected, and to contribute to the family. If you want your kid to talk, invite her in with short statements, say, "Tell me more," and solicit her opinion. You'll be having such stimulating two-way conversation that you won't even miss the old grunts, the eye rolls, and the previous misbehaviors.

Replay: Different Choices, Different Outcome

Remember those scenarios in the previous chapter? Let's replay each of them, now that you know what your children are thinking and how they're working you.

Scenario #1

Your nine-year-old wants to be in Little League this summer. You're all for it, but your husband isn't. Your kid pitches a fit and refuses to eat dinner.

WHAT THE AUTHORITARIAN PARENT WOULD DO

"You are *not* doing it. You're not good enough for us to spend the money. End of story. We're done talking here. If you're not going to eat, you can leave the table. I've had enough of this."

And he walks away, leaving his child frustrated.

WHAT THE PERMISSIVE PARENT WOULD DO

She would trail after the child as he left the table. "Honey, don't be upset. I think playing baseball is a great idea. I bet you'd be really good at it. Maybe even the best on the team. Let Dad cool down, okay? I'll go with you tomorrow and get you signed up."

Making the situation even more damaging, she might add, "And let's keep this between us. I can use some money that I have set aside, and your practices will be during the day when your dad is at work, so he won't really know. Once he sees you practicing in the yard and realizes how good you are, we can tell him what you're doing, and he'll be okay with it."

If the permissive parent is hard-core, she'll plead with her son, "Please come back and eat dinner." If he refuses and keeps heading for his room, she'll follow him and whisper, "I'll bring you something later, when your dad leaves for his meeting."

What the Authoritative Parent Would Do

You let the kid go to his room after pitching his fit. You and your spouse continue to eat dinner—more quietly now—and discuss next steps. By the time you've finished dinner, you have a plan, and you're unified in it.

You don't bring your son any dinner. He stays in his room and sulks that night.

The next day he approaches the parent he thinks will be easiest to bend to his wishes. Usually it's Mom. (Remember what I said about women being the highest percentage of pleasers?) But Mom is wise to his tactics this round. She gives the agreed-upon spiel when he begs again to be in Little League.

"I'm glad you're interested in a sport like baseball. This summer would be a good one to experiment. There's a group of boys who get together three times a week in the late afternoon at the nearby park. I can make room in my schedule to drive you there."

> Mom is wise to his tactics this round. She gives the agreed-upon spiel.

"But I want to play Little League," he whines. "All my friends are doing it."

"I understand. But we're not doing that this summer. You can play baseball with them other times, but not as part of Little League."

You well know that your son's interests change like the wind. He'd be tired of Little League after a couple of practices.

Still, your son kicks up the whine fest. "But why, Mom?"

Here's the teachable moment. "Because the scene you caused at dinner proved to us you're not mature enough to handle a sport like that on a regular basis."

Then you exit the room and let your son think about that for a while.

The next time he wants to do something like Little League, or anything else, he'll think a lot more about his approach. And since he's seen you two be a united force, he won't be as fast to play you against each other next time.

Scenario #2

Your 14-year-old and 16-year-old have a 10:30 bedtime but don't want to go to bed. They want to watch a movie, so they scheme together.

WHAT THE AUTHORITARIAN PARENT WOULD DO

"No. I said no, and I meant no. I shouldn't have to repeat myself. You get in your bedroom and stay there. And don't try any tricks either, or you won't be watching another movie for a year."

WHAT THE PERMISSIVE PARENT WOULD DO

"Of course you can stay up and watch a movie. It's good to have time with your siblings. But be in a good mood tomorrow when you see your father, or he'll blame it on staying up too late."

If the permissive parent is over the top, she'll add, "What movie do you guys want to watch? I've been thinking about getting a membership to Netflix. I guess tonight's a good night to start. I can even run to the store to get some snacks."

Problem is, it's a school night, and such enabling behavior won't help those kids pay attention in school tomorrow. Nor will it help them learn a lesson called patience. Good things come to those who wait.

WHAT THE AUTHORITATIVE PARENT WOULD DO

Since teaching responsibility is a critical part of good parenting, you have a couple of choices for how you could proceed.

Choice #1: "I understand you want to watch a video tonight, but it's a school night. Friday or Saturday is a much better option. I'll even throw in some homemade popcorn then. Now, though, it's time to retire to your rooms. Whether you choose to go to sleep or not is your business. But we all need this private time."

Choice #2: Let the older two play out their scheme, and play dumb so they leave the innocent younger one out of it. Retire to your room at your usual time and let them sneak out and watch the movie in your living room.

> Let the older two play out their scheme, and play dumb.

The next morning, secretly smile at the dark circles under their eyes and ignore their yawns. When they drag themselves in the door after school and want a nap instead of their usual snack, you can smile again. I bet anything those kids will go to bed early tonight.

It will probably be a while before they'll ask to watch a movie on a school night. And you didn't even have to say a thing.

Look how smart a parent you are.

Scenario #3

Your 12-year-old hates to do his chores, especially taking out the garbage. He conveniently forgets, stalls for time, or complains about doing it.

WHAT THE AUTHORITARIAN PARENT WOULD DO

"If you don't do your chores, you'll be grounded for life."

Or, "Something stinks around here, and it's not only your attitude. You get busy and do your job. No more stalling, no complaining. It's about time you do your share of the work around here."

Or, "Your *mother* had to take out the garbage today. Forget one more time and I'll make you regret it."

What the Permissive Parent Would Do

"It's okay. Everybody forgets sometimes. I know you're busy with school and other things. It's not a problem. I don't mind taking out the garbage."

What the Authoritative Parent Would Do

The garbage is *his* job, not yours. When it starts to get stinky in the kitchen, wheel that container right into his bedroom. Shut the door so it's fully aromatic by the time he gets back from school.

> The garbage is his job, not yours. When it starts to get stinky in the kitchen, wheel that container right into his bedroom.

When he opens his bedroom door, he'll get a surprise and come thundering back out into the kitchen. "What's with the garbage in my room?"

You shrug. "Oh, it was getting a little smelly in the kitchen."

"But why did you stick it in my room?" he asks angrily. "Are you crazy?"

You answer calmly, "It's your responsibility, so it belongs in your room until you take care of it."

End of subject. You get busy doing something else.

Besides providing a teachable moment for your son, you get a bonus. Your son actually cleans his bedroom since it really does reek in there.

Authoritative parenting is a win-win, isn't it?

Scenario #4

Your 16-year-old daughter has had a bad day at school. She got stabbed in the back by her best friend, and then a teacher gave her grief for her handwriting on a test. She wants to take it out on someone, but if she acts up at school, she'll get a reputation she doesn't want. She's got to fight with someone to let off steam, so she takes it out on you the instant she walks in the door.

What the Authoritarian Parent Would Do

"What's wrong with you?"

Or, "Why are you picking a fight with me? I'm your father."

Or, "Go to your room until your attitude improves."

Or, "Try this again, young lady, and you're in big trouble."

What the Permissive Parent Would Do

"Oh, honey, what's wrong? Can I help?"

Or, "Did you have a bad day? Did someone hurt you? If they did, I'll . . ."

And the permissive parent proceeds to follow her angry daughter down the hallway to try to help and gets caught in her teenager's wind.

What the Authoritative Parent Would Do

"I can see you've had a rough day. When you feel like talking about it, I'm all ears. Just come and find me."

Then you exit the room to a quieter spot.

You see, there's no fight if you don't engage. Fighting is an act of cooperation.

Believe me, that girl will talk when she feels like it, but in the meantime you won't be a punching bag for her heightened emotions. So let her have time to cool down, start to think more rationally about what happened that day, and maybe even get a snack. There's nothing like food to calm the beast—er, your teenager.

There's a fine line between parenting too much and parenting too little. Both take away the potential for teachable moments when your child can learn to make good choices, be responsible for her actions, and contribute to your family. After all, your end goal is to rear a balanced, forward-thinking adult who loves and respects you, is kind and generous, cares for others (including his siblings), respects authority, pulls his weight at work, and contributes in beneficial ways to make this planet a better place to live.

You can get there. Just continue reading.

Getting behind Your Child's Eyes

*What your child's life mantra is, how it developed,
and how it affects his or her behavior.*

"I'm at my wit's end," Stephanie confided. She's a mom of three, including two teenagers. "My kids always fight, but my 15-year-old is the worst. Each time we interact, I lose. She counters whatever I say and blasts me out of the water. I walk away feeling like a bad mom. I don't know what to do. She acts so much like . . . like . . ."

"Let me take a guess," I said when she struggled for words. "She acts like you?"

If you're the parent of a teen, accept that you'll be a ship riding out rocky seas for a while, and batten down the hatches against the gale-force winds that will inevitably blow. And if you have more than one teenager at a time, heaven help you.

But knowing a little secret helps: The kid you're most likely to clash with is the one most like you, and that clash has everything to do with birth order.

How well do you really know your child? What does she think? How does he feel? What bothers him? What does she resent about you? What motivates him?

To find out why your child is misbehaving, you have to get behind his eyes to see how he thinks, feels, and perceives events that happen to him, as well as the world in general. Understanding some basics about birth order, the life mantra it helps form, and how that translates into a lifestyle—including misbehaviors—is a good start.

Birth Order 101

Understanding how different birth orders experience life is a critical key to parenting each of your children in the way best suited to him or her, and to responding in a long-term beneficial way to their individual misbehaviors.

Firstborns: Dazzling Stars of the Family

You were the lucky recipient of *all* of your parents' attention for a while. Being the family guinea pig for Mom and Dad's parenting techniques had its perks and its disadvantages. The universe revolved around you. You were the first to do everything—walk, go potty by yourself, eat dirt, get your first grade, wear a bra, and go through driver's ed.

> The universe revolved around you.

Everything you did—right or wrong—was heightened, so you became an achiever, leader, and perfectionist. Because your parents' critical eye was trained on you, you are hard on others but hardest on yourself. You are logical and well organized, have a strong sense of justice, and take life seriously.

Books became your best friends, because you didn't have siblings for a while and only interacted with adults. Then those things called *siblings* arrived and you were held responsible for their misbehavior: "You're older. You ought to know better." With all the parental expectations heaped on you, no wonder you're a perfectionist.

What's your resulting life mantra? "I only count when I not only do things right but do them perfectly."

You're allergic to failure.

Only Children: Rocket Ships Poised to Take Off

If you're an only child, take all the qualities of a firstborn child and multiply them by three. That's you. You're everything a firstborn is but with extra doses of self-motivation, stress, and high achievement.

You think in black-and-white, use words like *always* and *never* liberally, and constantly raise the high bar on yourself. Nothing is ever good enough or perfect enough. You could do better. Even the thought of failing at anything skyrockets your stress. You are triply allergic to failure.

> You are triply allergic to failure.

What's your resulting life mantra? "I only count when I'm perfect."

Middleborns: Diplomats in the Making

You're smarter than your parents give you credit for. You took one look at your older brother or sister and decided, *No way can I compete with that.*

So you went in the opposite direction. You became independent and secretive and decided that it's best if you don't share what you really think. Squished between firstborn star and entertaining baby, you mediated between the two warring parties as the family diplomat enough that you learned to retreat at the first sign of a fight brewing.

Wanting life's roads to be smooth, you avoid conflicts and compromise rather than provoke a fight. You're often elusive in your answers—"We'll see . . ."—instead of stating yes or no.

You avoid conflicts and compromise rather than provoke a fight.

Since you were least likely to be noticed as missing from the dinner table, you're actually surprised when anyone in your family pays attention to you. That's why you've majored on developing your friend network, and you're very loyal.

What's your resulting life mantra? "I only count when I can keep the peace and slip under the radar."

Lastborns: Master Charmers and Manipulators

Engaging, impulsive, and affectionate, you love people, activities, and surprises. You're not only comfortable with but crave being in the limelight as the center of attention. After all, you grew up as the baby, the apple of Mama's and Papa's eyes. You were the entertainer, the party waiting to happen, the one who made everyone laugh.

But you sometimes dodged responsibility. Since you were "cute," your siblings often got blamed for what you did because they were older, should have known better, and let you get in trouble.

However, they got their revenge on you. When your siblings wanted something from your parents, they used you as the token sacrifice. After all, who could say no to you? As the youngest, you were the one less likely to get killed.

You're allergic to work. It's much easier to charm someone else into doing it.

What's your resulting life mantra? "I only count when I'm noticed and I can make people laugh."

You're allergic to work. It's much easier to charm someone else into doing it.

Smart Parenting Based on Birth Order

Just as these characteristics are likely true of you (see my *Birth Order Book* for more specifics and reasons for variations), they're also true of your child, and that's where the clashing occurs. There's no such thing as treating your kids equally. You'll over-identify with the child of the same birth order as you—putting too much pressure on her or favoring her too much. That actually *provokes* misbehavior on the part of your kids. How does this play out in real life?

Take the number one scenario parents across the globe complain about: fighting kids. How do you usually respond? Has that worked in the past 15 years? Then why not try these strategies?

Firstborns make snap decisions about who's at fault and level immediate punishments. Either you hold your firstborn responsible because she's oldest and ought to know better (even though you hated when your parents said that to you), or your critical eye zooms in on the baby, since your little brother got away with murder. You jump in to solve problems because you like issues defined and settled, and because your firstborn teen has the same black-and-white thinking and sense of justice, you two will understandably butt heads.

You be the adult. Be the first not to engage in the fight.

Onlies spout an infamous line: "Can't you all just get along?" But competition and sibling rivalry are natural and, frankly, as unavoidable as death and taxes. Give up that ideal, stay out of the fracas, and let them tussle it out.

Middleborns hate disharmony, so they step in to smooth things over—"Now, kids, what is this all about?"—and make the complaint fest worse. You jump to the middleborn's defense, since you know what it's like to be sandwiched in the middle of a mess you didn't create. But don't needlessly get involved in your kids' fights. Realize that fighting is an act of *cooperation* (it takes two or more), and let *them* problem solve. Encourage your conflict-avoiding middleborn to stand up for himself.

Babies swoop in like avenging angels to defend the youngest: "Why are you picking on your sister? What did she ever do to you?" Yes, you got away with a lot yourself, but you remember your siblings pounding on you when Mom wasn't looking. Don't make the cardinal mistake of baby-of-the-family parents: targeting the firstborn because she's the oldest. I guarantee your littlest angel helped fuel that conflict and needs a liberal dose of responsibility.

> Fights fizzle when you don't fight back or act as judge between the two parties.

It's amazing how swiftly fights fizzle when your kids can't get your attention and you don't fight back or act as judge between the two parties.

Parenting is not a competitive sport. If someone is "winning" your relationship, you're both losing.

Getting Inside Your Child's Head

"My sister is both my BFF and my worst enemy," 13-year-old Mona told me. "When no one understands why I'm upset, she gets it. I don't have to explain. But I really hate how she's in my business—telling me what to do and how I should feel. She's only two years older, but she acts like such a know-it-all, wannabe princess. Worse, my parents give her everything. Sometimes she's too . . . perfect."

"It could be worse," I said. "You could be stuck between that perfect sister and a little show-off brother, who gets away with everything."

But I knew exactly how she felt, because I had *two* perfect older siblings. My straight-A sister always had her ducks in a row, and my captain-of-the-football-team brother could do no wrong. Then there was me—that show-off brother. Nobody took me seriously, and everybody told me what to do.

Again, misbehavior is *purposive*—there's a reason for it. Now that I understand a few secrets about why people do what they do, I know why each of us acted like we did.

Birth order has a powerful effect on how your kids view you, themselves, and their siblings and how you all relate to each other. If you get behind your child's eyes to see what they're *really* thinking, you can halt some misbehavior before it starts and get in the driver's seat to curb it.

> If you get behind your child's eyes to see what they're really *thinking,* you can halt some misbehavior before it starts.

Want to know what your firstborn, onlyborn, middleborn, and lastborn are thinking? Let's take a look.

What Your Firstborn Is Really Thinking . . .

It's so unfair. If my little sister does something wrong, why am I the one who gets in trouble? If I had a buck for every time Dad said, "You have to be a role model," I'd be a millionaire by now.

I'm always under pressure, because Mom and Dad watch me closely. I feel like if I don't make captain of the volleyball team, I'll be a failure in their eyes. And if I get a B instead of an A, watch out. The world is going to end.

Sometimes I need space to myself, to process things or read a book or listen to music, but I get interrupted. My little brother and sister don't know what a closed door means, and they get into my private stuff and make a mess. When I tell them to get out and stay out of my stuff, they run crying to Mom and I get in trouble for not being nicer to them. I don't play with their toys, so why should they get to play with mine—and break them?

I also have to do extra chores because I'm older. I mean, why on earth can't my little brother feed our dog? He's in second grade. And why do I have to be the one to babysit when Mom and Dad go out for dinner? Especially when it messes with the plans I've made?

At my house, I'm the garbage person—the one who not only takes out the garbage but does every single garbage thing that my brother and sister can't seem to do because they're younger.

At my house, I'm the garbage person—the one who not only takes out the garbage but does every single garbage thing that my brother and sister can't seem to do because they're younger. Can't somebody else help out around here? I have enough stress with my schoolwork and trying to do well, not to mention trying not to get eaten alive in the jungle of school every day. And then I get grounded for having an attitude? Who wouldn't have an attitude if you were treated like that?

What You Can Do for Your Firstborn

Knowing what your firstborn is thinking can make her misbehaviors less "personal." After all, if you were the one under all that stress, wouldn't you lose your temper every once in a while and slam your bedroom door or say something not very courteous?

A helpful conversation to have with your firstborn might go something like this: "I know you live with a lot of pressure as a firstborn. Between school, all your extra activities, and your pesky brother and sister, you've got a lot to handle."

Already you have her attention. She's thinking, *Wait a minute. Dad knows I have to deal with a lot and that my siblings can be a nuisance?* All of a sudden her ears are open to hear what you have to say.

You continue. "I also know you have a lot of chores to do. I've been thinking about lessening some of those as your schoolwork is growing, and I'd like to hear your opinion on that."

Her ears open wider since you asked for her opinion.

"I'll be honest. There's a reason you have so many chores. Think about it this way: If you wanted to get something done, would you call on someone you know is responsible, or the person who can't find her shoes in the morning—like your sister? The fact we call on you and don't follow through to check up is because we believe in you. But I don't think it's fair that you have to shoulder so many responsibilities, so I'd like you to work with me on teaching some of them to your brother and sister. If you could make a list of chores you think they could do and make some suggestions, that would be great."

You've complimented her on being responsible and reassured her of your belief in her. Remember, firstborns are organized and detailed and love lists, so she'll hop right on this project.

You end your conversation with a positive twist: "I know your brother and sister can be annoying. But they really look up to you. They think you walk on water, so that's why they like to hang around you and learn from you. You're cool, and you get to do things they can't do. They're curious about your stuff, which is why they invade your room. So, in a funny way, the fact they get into your stuff is actually a compliment. After all, you rock!

"But you don't have to be right or perfect all the time. You're human too. We'll always love you and support you. We believe in you."

That, parent, is a fabulous start to a changed relationship that could end your firstborn's misbehaviors.

TIPS FOR PARENTING
Firstborns

- Realize they live with a lot of pressure and responsibility. Give them a break. They can't always be perfect.
- Don't blame siblings' misbehavior on them.
- Insist younger siblings hold up their end in family chores.
- Take the time to lay things out in detail.
- Give your firstborn some space without you or their siblings in it.
- Don't treat them as your instant babysitter. Before assuming they can do it, check in to see if their schedule allows for some babysitting later in the day, that evening, or that weekend. In other words, treat them with respect and they'll return it.
- Recognize their special place in the family. As the oldest, they should get special privileges to go along with the additional responsibilities that come their way.
- Don't pile on more responsibilities. Make sure the younger ones are also pulling their weight.
- Watch your criticism. Don't jump in with a correction. For example, if your firstborn is reading to you and has trouble with a word, allow him time to sound it out. Give help only when he asks for it. Firstborns are extremely sensitive to criticism and being corrected.
- Make sure you have one-on-one or two-on-one time—just your oldest child with one or both parents. Firstborns respond better to adult company than middleborns or lastborns do, and they crave it because they had it before their siblings joined the family. So make a special effort to take your firstborn out alone for a treat or to run an errand.

What Your Onlyborn Is Really Thinking . . .

Life is stressful if I don't have a road map. I like to know where I'm going and when I'm getting there, including the details. It drives me crazy if I don't know, because then I can't strategize.

That's why I spend extra time on my homework and study extra hard for tests.

I hate it when my parents pressure me about grades or studying. I'm already under a lot of pressure. It's not like I wouldn't study. But it makes me feel like they don't trust me because I'm a kid.

I hate it even more when they make decisions for me, like I'm too dumb to do it myself. The other day Dad came into my room without permission and sorted through my college brochures. At dinner, he presented three of them labeled with #1, #2, and #3 and told me he'd evaluated the best schools for me.

There is absolutely no way I'm going to any of those schools . . . just because he picked them. It's my life, not his. Why is he messing in my business? He had his time to consider colleges. Now it's mine. But telling him that didn't go over so well.

"I'm only thinking of your best," Dad said.

Well, so am I. Can't I be allowed a say in my own future? It isn't my fault I'm their only kid and I have to carry on the honor of the family name.

> Can't I be allowed a say in my own future? It isn't my fault I'm their only kid and I have to carry on the honor of the family name.

I also get sick of them saying, "Why don't you act more friendly, and then you'd get some friends?" I do have friends—a few, but they're good ones. I'm not a social nitwit, but I don't like being with other kids all the time. I'd rather spend time alone with my books and do something every once in a while. My friends are like that too.

Even though I'm their only kid, do Mom and Dad have to keep such close tabs on me? Sometimes I want to relax, but I feel like I can't. One of them says, "You should . . ." They won't stop pushing me to do something else or do something better.

I feel like I'm never good enough for them. Like the time I was a kid and made my bed all by myself. I was so proud that I asked Mom to come look at it. She said, "Good job, honey," but then smoothed out some wrinkles and remade one corner. Or when I had learned how to read by kindergarten and was struggling with a word, and she said, "Don't you know that word yet?" I mean, seriously, most of the other kids in kindergarten were still eating paste.

See what I mean? They're so critical, when I'm already hard enough on myself.

The only way to get around them is to act on the surface like I'm doing what they want. Then as soon as I go out the door, I can do whatever *I* want.

I rarely get caught. When I do, I get hammered way harder than my friends, who do something far worse. But I know if I wait long enough, my parents will get over it, and I can go back to business as usual under the radar.

What You Can Do for Your Onlyborn

Knowing what your only child is thinking can make his misbehaviors less "personal." They also hit home a bit too, don't they?

He is your only child, so you have a lot of hopes and dreams staked on that kid. You have his best in mind, but sometimes the way you act out your parental expectations adds more weight to an only child's already heavy burden. It's no surprise then that your only child sometimes throws a few words in your face like:

- "Would you get off my back? I'm trying my best here."
- "I know it's a Thursday night. I only went out for a bit to get some fresh air, but you act like I'm going to fail my test tomorrow if I take a break."
- "Stop interfering and let me handle it!"

> **TIPS FOR PARENTING**
> ### Onlies
>
> - Give them a break. They can't always be perfect. Realize they live with a lot of pressure and responsibility as the torchbearer for the family.
> - Watch your critical eye. They already have two on themselves—their own—and don't need yours added to it.
> - Don't "should" on them ("You should do this"). They already do that enough to themselves. Giving the double whammy will make them resent you, lower their self-worth, and make them harder to deal with.
> - Don't improve on what they say or do. It only reinforces their already ingrained perfectionism. Accept the slightly wrinkled bed, the not-quite-cleaned room, or whatever else they've done. If you do it over, you send the message that they aren't measuring up to your expectations.
> - Take the time to lay things out in detail for them.
> - Give them quiet space without intruding.
> - Realize they feel more comfortable with adults than with their own peers, so they may make friends slowly. The good thing is, the friends they do make are usually keepers, while most other kids change friends as frequently as they change shirts.

A helpful conversation to have with your only child might go something like this: "I understand now how much pressure we put on you, and I'm sorry."

That initial statement will get his attention, especially since you, his almighty parent, have said the words "I'm sorry." To onlyborns, saying that is like magic dust.

"You do so incredibly well at everything in life, and you already drive yourself hard. By saying some of the things I have, I know it's made you feel even more stressed. So if you'll help me, I want to back off. I'm going to try to catch myself before I remind you of things you already know or ask you about homework. After all, you've already got it, and you're even more detailed than we are.

"But I also want you to know that even if you failed a test, it wouldn't change my view of you. I'm sorry I've been critical of you in the past and put extra pressure on you. If there is anything I can do to help you or ease your burden, I'm all ears. I know I will still make mistakes. You'll make mistakes. Neither of us is perfect, and that's okay. But I'd like to start over, from this point on, with you and me. Could you help me do that?"

"I'm sorry" is a critical first step toward an onlyborn, who feels pressure every day of his life. When he knows you care about him, understand him, and want to make changes, a bit of that internal stress will roll off him. But an onlyborn will also wait to see if your actions line up with your words.

It'll take time, but now you'll at least be traversing the same terrain as your child.

What Your Middleborn Is Really Thinking . . .

Sometimes I wonder what I'm doing here in my family. Nobody even notices if I'm not at dinner. It's like I'm invisible. If I took off, it would probably be days before they'd even miss me.

I've spent my entire existence squished between my perfect older brother, who can do no wrong, and my bratty sister, who gets attention no matter what she does because she's "cute." The best way to survive is to keep my mouth shut and let the fireworks happen around me. When my brother and sister fight, I lay low as long as I can. But often I'm the one who gets called on to step between them. I end up having to negotiate some peace when all I want is some quiet space for myself and peace in the house.

No one ever asks what I think. Even if they did and I tried to answer, they probably couldn't hear me with all the noise my little sister makes. Honestly, sometimes I feel like an alien in my own family. I don't belong.

That's why my friends are so important to me. If I'm having a bad day, I shut my door and text them. They feel more like family than my family does. My parents don't get that, and there's no way I can tell them. So I continue getting into trouble for missing curfew so I can hang out longer with my friends.

> *No one ever asks what I think. Even if they did and I tried to answer, they probably couldn't hear me with all the noise my little sister makes.*

What You Can Do for Your Middleborn

Knowing what your middleborn is thinking can make her misbehaviors less "personal." After all, if you were the one caught in the middle of your siblings' battles, and you felt like you were invisible and ignored in your family, wouldn't you get in trouble every now and then to show them you existed?

A helpful conversation to have with your middleborn might go something like this: "I'd love to have your help on something. I'm trying to figure out how to launch a website for my new business, but I'm running into trouble. You're so good at figuring out online things. I see you on your computer all the time, and you seem like a whiz. Do you think you could help me out?"

Because middleborns feel invisible, asking for their opinion or help on something is like stroking a kitten—the right way, of course. Stroke them the wrong direction, ruffle their fur, and you've got an angry kitten.

As you are working on the project together, say, "I know how important your friends are to you and how much you enjoy spending time with them. I'd love to hear your ideas about how you could still get that time with them but also weave in some more time for us as a family. I know that at this stage in your life, you don't always want to have Mom or Dad around. But I was thinking lately that I don't get enough time with you. I miss you when you're not around."

Her ears perk up. *Mom finally gets how important my friends are to me? But she misses me? What's going on here?*

"I'd love to do something fun with you. Just you and me, not the other kids. Are there some things you'd like to do without dragging the other kids along? If you come up with some suggestions, I'd love to hear them."

By now your middleborn is in shock. *Get rid of the other kids for the night and do something fun?*

"Hey, I know it's hard being stuck in the middle all the time between those two. Your brother's usually getting an award for something or other, and your sister, well . . ." You laugh. "She has to call attention to herself if she doesn't get attention, doesn't she?"

TIPS FOR PARENTING
Middleborns

- Realize they will avoid conflict. That's why they disappear frequently.
- Solicit their opinion or advice. They're used to being invisible, so they won't speak first and they won't speak up for themselves.
- Take extra care to make them feel special, especially since they're squeezed between their brothers and sisters.
- Show interest in what's important to them, including their friends and activities.
- Thank them for putting out the fires in family fights.
- Spend one-on-one time with them. Since middleborns avoid sharing their feelings, set aside talking time for the

two of you. Though it's important to do that with every child, a middle child is least likely to insist on their fair share. Be sure they get it.

- Set up some regular privileges your middleborn can count on. Maybe it's something as simple as watching a certain TV show every week with no interference from anyone else in the family. Maybe it's going to a certain restaurant every month with just you. What's important is that whatever the privilege is, it's the middle child's *exclusive* territory.

- Make sure they get new items of clothing, not only hand-me-downs from an older sibling. For families with sufficient income this may not be a problem, but in some homes hand-me-downs are a regular part of growing up. An occasional one is fine, but your middle child will be particularly appreciative of something new, especially a key item like a jacket or pair of jeans.

- When faced with misbehavior, listen carefully to their answers or explanations. Their desire to avoid conflict and not make waves may get in the way of the real facts. They're loyal to friends so don't want them to get in trouble, even if they have to take the blame themselves. You may have to prod gently, "I know what you're saying, but I feel like there's more behind it than that. I'd like to have the whole story. I want to know what really happened and how you feel about it. You won't get in trouble, so you can be honest."

- Above all, be sure the family photo album has its share of pictures of your middle child. Don't let him fall victim to the stereotypical fate of seeing thousands of pictures of his older sibling and only a few of him. Also, take pictures of your middle child by himself, not as a part of his siblings. By doing so, you're saying to your middle child, "*You* are unique and important to me."

She nods. *Wow, she knows what it's like to be in my shoes.*

"That's why I appreciate you so much. You're the even-keeled one in our family, the kid I can count on. You get along well with both of your siblings. When they fight—and they do fight a lot, don't they?—you don't pick sides. You're a master negotiator. Maybe you can be a diplomat someday. You're so good at seeing all sides of an issue and getting them to stop fighting. Your brother and sister need you more than they know. It's the reason they run to you in the first place. They see that you, and only you, know how to solve the issue."

Hey, she really gets it, and yeah, I am good at that.

"But don't forget," you conclude, "you have a right to express your opinion too. What you think and feel matter. They matter greatly to me and to your dad. When you're not around, we miss you. So I'd love to find a win-win solution where you get time with your friends and we have time with you."

Do that, parent, and you've redirected your middleborn's misbehavior of constantly missing curfew and getting in trouble. You've now given her reasons to come home.

Above all else, middleborns need to know that they matter and what they think is important. Little things you do mean a great deal.

One night years ago I took all three of our kids bowling. As we sat down to start our score sheet, there was an intense discussion over who would bowl first. While Holly, my firstborn, and Kevin II, my baby of the family, vied loudly for the honor, I noticed Krissy, my middleborn, wasn't saying a word.

"Krissy," I said, "you get to choose."

What did Krissy do? What middleborn children would—keep the peace like true diplomats. She put down her daddy's name first, then Holly, then Kevin II, and finally herself.

But she also smiled because her daddy had solicited her opinion.

What Your Lastborn Is Really Thinking . . .

Do they have any idea how hard it is to grow up with a perfect older sister? I get compared all the time to her, so I've given up. I'll never get As or be on the student council like her.

And my popular older brother? Don't even get me started. I get so tired of people saying, "Oh, you're Jett's brother. So do you play soccer too?" Duh, just because we're related doesn't mean we're alike.

But when I want people to notice me, I know exactly how to get their attention. I'm good at it too. I can get Mom to show up at school and get me out early if I do things like crawl under the bathroom stalls and lock them from inside, or pour my milk into another kid's backpack. A short trip to the principal's office is nothing compared to getting out of school early and Mom taking me to Taco Bell on the way home because she didn't have a lunch planned.

When my perfect sister is driving me crazy, I know how to get her in trouble: I "accidentally" drop her phone in the toilet. When she screams and comes after me, she's the one who gets in trouble the most because she's older. Besides, my yelling attracts Mom's and Dad's attention more, because I can yell louder. They come running like trained dogs.

But she also knows how to get back at me. When she wants to weasel a favor out of our parents without getting killed, she sends me to ask. I'm game. After all, I have a much higher chance of getting what she wants, and there's usually something in it for me. Last time she gave me five bucks because I got them to sign up for YouTube Red.

I've also got my sister's number. If I don't want to do something, I act cute or incapable and she takes care of it for me. Even if she calls me "stupid" or "loser," it doesn't matter.

My brother's so busy with his friends that he basically ignores me, except for when my sister and I get in a fight at home. Then he tells us both to shut up or Mom and Dad will hear.

But I'm not smart like my sister or as popular as my brother, so I have to make Mom and Dad pay attention to me somehow. If I act up, I get their attention. If I don't, nobody will notice me.

So, let's see. What should I do next to get some attention around here? Throw those leftover jelly donuts at passing cars? Tie the cat to our backyard tree? Shave the neighbor's dog? He might look good with a crew cut on one side. . . .

What should I do next to get some attention around here? Throw those leftover jelly donuts at passing cars? Tie the cat to our backyard tree? Shave the neighbor's dog?

What You Can Do for Your Lastborn

Knowing what your lastborn is thinking can make his misbehaviors less "personal." If you viewed his behavior as a way to get attention since he can't compete with his perfect sister, would that change your response to it? Realizing his life mantra is "I only count when people pay attention to me and I can make them laugh," do you now understand his clown behavior that otherwise would drive you crazy?

A helpful conversation to have with your lastborn might go something like this: "Your sister is sometimes over the top, isn't she?"

Your lastborn's ears perk up. *What? Mom thinks so too?*

"I mean, she's good at so many things, but she takes herself way too seriously at times. I wouldn't be surprised if that bothers you sometimes."

What a minute. Mom understands what I think and how I feel?

"But you know what? As irritated as the two of you get with each other, you still need each other. She needs you to make her laugh when she's stressed out. And you need her, even when she's high-and-mighty sometimes. Remember when she rescued you from the neighborhood bully by reading him the riot act so he got scared and ran away? And then he never bothered you again?"

He nods, and you relive that experience with laughter.

"Well," you continue, "that's the same sister whose phone you chose to drop in the toilet yesterday. As a result, she missed a very important call from a college about an interview."

You let that sink in for a moment. Now his head is hanging a bit.

"I'm sorry, Mom."

"You don't need to apologize to me. Apologize to your sister."

"Okay," he says meekly.

"I also know that sometimes she does your chores, and I don't think that's fair to her or to you."

Shoot, he thinks. *Mom noticed.*

"You don't like it when your brother and sister treat you like a baby, right? Well, a little work won't kill you, and it'll make them take you more seriously. You're a member of this family, just like your sister, your brother, your dad, and me. We all work together and play together. That means you need to do the work assigned to you instead of letting your sister do it.

"I know you like to make people laugh, and I love that about you. But sometimes your brother and sister also need a place in the spotlight, to be applauded for their accomplishments. You don't need to do something like drop your sister's phone in the toilet to get our attention. You always have it. If you don't feel like that and you want some attention, come up to me or Dad and say, 'I need to talk,' or 'I need a hug,' or 'I'm feeling bored right now.' Those are good solutions to wanting attention."

TIPS FOR PARENTING
Lastborns

- Let them entertain you. They're good at it.
- Pay attention to their positive behaviors and you'll have fewer misbehaviors.
- Don't fall for their manipulative charms and do their work for them. Make sure they carry out their fair share of responsibilities around the house. Lastborns often wind up with very little to do for two reasons: (1) They are masters at ducking out of work to be done, and (2) they are so little and "helpless" that the rest of the family members decide it's easier to do the work themselves than to make sure the babies follow through on what they're supposed to do.
- Don't let them get away with murder. The lastborn is the least likely in the family to be disciplined and the least likely to have to meet parental expectations the way the older children do. So think, *How did I hold the older kids responsible? What time did I have them go to bed when they were that age?* Then enforce similar rules for the lastborn. Don't let him get away scot-free with a fantasyland experience because you're too tired to parent anymore.
- Don't coddle them, but don't let them get clobbered or lost in the shuffle either. Lastborns are well known for feeling "Nothing I do is important," so it's no wonder they don't try very hard. Make a big deal out of their accomplishments (remember, they crave the limelight), and make sure they get their fair share of space on the refrigerator door with school papers, drawings, and rewards.
- Introduce them to reading very early. Six months isn't too young to start reading to them with brightly colored illustrated books. When they start reading, don't do the work for them of sounding out words. Lastborns like to be read to and will let you do most of the work if they can get away with it. That's why they are often the latest ones to read in the family and are also the poorest readers. They'd rather

socialize any day than read a book. Socializing is as natural as breathing air. Reading is work.

- Call their bluff when you need to, including misbehaviors. Give them choices: "Do your homework tonight and watch your favorite TV program later, or don't do your homework and don't watch that program later." Or, "Shape up at school or drop baseball. Your choice. No pressure."
- Treat them with respect and they'll rise to the challenge, even if sometimes they have to get nudged a bit.
- Complete their baby book before they're 21. Yes, life piles up with the arrival of that third child (or more). No, you don't have as much time as you used to. But that child still needs your positive attention. Let other things go, like the dusting or that promotion at work, to provide time for your baby.

Taking the Long View

You knew your kids were different, but now you understand even more *why* they are different. That's why you should never treat your kids the same, because they *aren't* the same. Trying to treat them that way only provokes rebellion.

Once you understand how birth order affects your thinking and your child's and prompts your child's misbehaviors, you'll be better equipped to deal with those misbehaviors. Sure, they will still rear their heads. Siblings will fight. That's as sure as gravity. They'll compete even more if they're only a couple of years apart and the same gender. But if you think of that fighting as something else—an act of cooperation in getting your attention—you won't be as tempted to engage and escalate the fight, will you?

Want to take the wind out of your kid's sails if she tries to narc on her sister? Just say, "Wow, you could be right," and walk away. Or when siblings are in each other's faces and trying to loop you in, shrug and say, "Well, I'm sure you'll work it out," and exit the room.

Keeping the long-term perspective in mind is critically important in parenting. Tempers may heat up, but they'll blow over.

Here's some irony about siblings: In the morning, brother and sister might hate each other and go head-to-head in battle. But if another kid tries to pick on that sister at school, guess who goes to bat for her? Yup, her brother, the same one she called a "colossal pain" hours earlier. Why is he first in line to defend her? Because that's what family does.

Want to Know What Your Kid Is Really Thinking?

If you want to know what your child is really thinking, shut up and listen.

If you're the typical parent, when your kid comes to you with a problem, you know how they should feel and how they shouldn't feel. You think you're being helpful when you say things like:

- "Oh, honey, it'll be okay. Don't worry about it."
- "It's not that big of a thing."
- "You're too sensitive."
- "I'm sure it'll get better."
- "Are you sure you're not imagining it?"
- "This too shall pass."
- "It can't be that bad!"

But all those seemingly helpful statements convey that you didn't hear their heart. That kid risked sharing with you something real and intimate that's authentically bothering them, and you minimized the importance of that drama.

What is your kid really thinking? *Well, I tried to bring up something very important to these people who say they love me more* than anything, and what do they say? *"Don't worry about it! It's not a big deal."* They're not the ones getting called *"Pizza Face"* at school. So what will your kid do? He'll back away from you like you're a hot potato, flee to his room, and slam the door. Then he'll turn to his semi-confused peer group for advice.

If you really want to know what your child is thinking, you have to get behind his eyes to view his world from his perspective. To do that, you have to be available and ease into the potential conversation by saying something like, "Looks like you had a rough day. I'll be here if you want to talk."

With such an open invitation, that kid will talk—eventually. When he does, become a masterful listener with the following three tips.

Realize feelings aren't right or wrong.

They're just feelings. You don't like others telling you how you should feel, so why would you do that to your child?

Don't judge or minimize the drama.

Keep your listening hat on and your mouth shut—except for comments like, "I can see why that hurt" or "Tell me more."

Grow a "third ear" in the middle of your forehead.

Set aside any work you're doing and engage actively. Listen to their words. Watch for the emotion that flashes across their face.

Whenever your child is brave enough to share something with you, she's saying, "I trust you with my deepest feelings and thoughts." If you have a kid like that, I applaud you because you must already be a good listener. If your kid tends to clam up, though, it's not too late to turn your relationship around. You be the adult and say, "I haven't been very good at listening to you, but I want to get better at it. Would you be kind enough to help me?"

After the initial shock passes, I doubt a kid on the planet would turn that down. That's because, even when it doesn't seem like it, you are the most important constant in your child's rapidly evolving universe.

The Four Stages of Misbehavior

*What they are, how they start, and how to
identify where your child is on the spectrum.*

I used to have a dog that had a mind of her own. Barkley was a cocker spaniel, and she got herself into all kinds of trouble. "Unpredictable" was her middle name. Once she got something in that doggie head of hers, it lodged there until it was taken care of. You could tell her no, but you well knew she'd do it anyway. Once when we were in the middle of dinner, she sneaked up behind us, grabbed the meatloaf off the table, and ran off with it.

Another time we were working on a puzzle. She stole a piece, hightailed it down the hallway, and hid it somewhere. That puzzle piece still hasn't come up for air, and my wife is a very good housekeeper.

Those two events provoke laughter at the family dinner table now, but at the time they weren't so funny. We were minus our delicious main dish and left with only asparagus and potatoes. Salami lunch meat wasn't a good substitute. Pieces of that meatloaf also fell off as Barkley ran and made a big mess on the carpet. And regarding that missing puzzle piece, there's nothing more irritating than not being able to complete the masterpiece you've worked on as a family for a month.

When that dog didn't get the strokes from us that she wanted, when she wanted them, she created situations that would make us pay attention to her.

Your Kids' Game Plan

Your kids are the same way. All misbehavior is a call for attention. If your child doesn't get attention from you through positive actions, he'll proceed to making you pay attention through negative actions. That misbehavior will continue as long as it pays off. When it no longer gains him anything, he'll stop. The faster you pay the right kind of attention, the better off you'll be.

> All misbehavior is a call for attention. The faster you pay the right kind of attention, the better off you'll be.

Kids develop their game plan by watching you. How you respond to situations life throws your way role-models for them how they should respond. Your children are always making notes, figuring out how to get what they want, when they want it. And, parent, they're masterful at identifying all your hot buttons, how to push them, and how to work you. Every time they learn something new, they'll tuck it away and use it when needed to their advantage.

Children are influenced by creature comforts. That's why a baby cries when she's hungry or there are doodies in her diaper. And she'll fuss, like that baby did in the restaurant when she didn't like sitting in that cold, hard high chair and preferred sitting in a warm, cushy lap. She was only trying to make life more comfy for herself. As she went along in life, she was learning from her parents' responses, *Oh, so they're big on that. I see. How can I use that?*

Parent, once you're big on something, watch out. That item will become a lightning rod for your child.

- Grades are big to you, huh? Well, watch this . . .
- You don't like it when I fuss in front of other big people, do you? Hmm, I can get what I want if I . . .
- You hate being embarrassed in front of your friends? Have I got a new one for you . . .
- You can't stand it when anyone questions you? So if I . . .

Those are only the beginning.

That's why the parents of that baby should have insisted she stay in her own seat. "I have a seat, Dad has a seat, Grandma has a seat, and you have a seat. We all stay in our own seats at dinner." If the baby chose not to eat her own food, so be it. Natural hunger kicks in sooner or later, and the kid will eat.

Of course, following those steps for a child who has already discovered the power in her little finger would temporarily cause a big fuss. The family might not want to go back to that restaurant for a while. In fact, takeout or cooking at home would be a better option as they retrain their daughter. But sometimes you have to face down a bit of embarrassment to do what's right for the long term.

What's Real to Your Child

Kids react to the social environment in which they're placed and to whatever is going on around them. That's how they learn.

Your child's reality is based on what he believes he sees and what he believes he hears. These can be real or imagined perceptions.

Have you ever seen one of those optical illusion pictures where what one person sees is different from what another person sees? Well, what one kid in your family perceives to be real can be completely different from what another kid perceives to be real. That's why siblings often remember key family events differently.

For example, an older sibling remembers the awful Christmas he had when he was 13. The whole family was snowed in, and he was forced to play with his little brother during "family bonding time" instead of reading the books he'd set aside. To top it off, his parents gave him and his brother the same present—sleds. It would have been a nice present, back when he was five or six.

> *Your child's reality is based on what he believes he sees and what he believes he hears.*

Little brother remembers that same Christmas as the best ever. The whole family was together, they got to make snow angels, and he made up a Christmas play and everybody acted in it. He got a red sled too, and he and his brother spent time sledding down that hill once the snow cleared.

Exact same event, but viewed through completely different lenses.

Why such a differing perception? Because the way each child viewed reality based on his birth order, parental responses to his actions, and his experiences thus far shaped his memories.

The older brother was serious and had grown up under his parents' high expectations. He'd looked forward to some downtime from school, a letup of pressure, and reading good books he wouldn't have had time to read otherwise. Instead, he was forced into being social and received a present that insulted his age and his intelligence.

The younger brother loved having the family gathered around and being snowed in. It was exciting, and everybody paid attention to him instead of ignoring him like usual. They even let him make up his own Christmas play and star in it. To top it off, the brother who usually called him "Dumbo" took him outside and went sledding with him. They even had a snowball fight. What could be better?

That Christmas, one of those two boys got in trouble for his misbehavior. Can you guess which one it was?

You're right. It was the older brother, who had never been in trouble before. The younger brother got off scot-free and had a Disney World–type vacation.

What did the older brother hear from his parents? A litany of these comments:

- "What's wrong with you? All we're asking is for you to play with your brother for once."
- "What's with the attitude? You've had a terrible attitude this entire break."
- "You're always in your room. We're a family, and this is family time."
- "Your brother created a Christmas play, and everybody needs to act in it. Let's go."
- "I can't believe you smacked your brother in the face with a snowball that had a rock in the middle. How could you do that? Now he's crying."
- "I thought you were the good kid, but you're showing your true colors. What a Christmas."

Yes, he was thinking, *what a Christmas indeed. It's the worst time in my life. And nobody even noticed my all-As report card or congratulated me on finishing that month-long state history paper that I did tons of research on. Everything is all about my brother, as usual.*

Can you see why that once-perfect child rebelled? He didn't get attention for the positive things he was doing and was frustrated with all the attention his annoying younger brother was getting. He decided the only way to get any attention himself was to put a rock in a snowball and launch it at his brother. Maybe then his family might have a clue how angry and disappointed he was about his "vacation" being ruined.

I would have rebelled too in those circumstances and done much worse. So would you, unless you're a saint.

Why Kids Misbehave

Of course, I wouldn't know what it was like to be perfect, since I was that little brother, the family clown and troublemaker. By the time I was 13, I'd done so many antics an entire book couldn't list them all. I only gave authority a lick and a holler. I always called home and told my parents where I was because I knew I was supposed to. Problem was, I was never where I said. But because my parents fell for it, I didn't have to rope my buddy Moonhead into vouching for me.

Why did I spend my childhood misbehaving? Because that was the only way I could get attention. I wasn't my perfect straight-A-student older sister, and I wasn't my perfect sports-star, popular older brother. So I became the family clown.

Kids misbehave for a reason. The idea that behavior has a purpose was first stated by psychiatrist Alfred Adler, who was a practical guy but wrote very thick books. So that more people could understand Adler's principles about behavior, a student of his, Dr. Rudolf Dreikers, organized them into four goals: attention, power, revenge, and display of inadequacy. Researchers Don Dinkmeyer and Gary McKay simplified Adler's theories further by providing a chart of these "4 Goals of Misbehavior."[5]

What's most critical to know is that these goals are sequential. Simply stated, if kids can't get your attention in a positive way and become discouraged, they move to the next stage: getting your attention through powerful, negative behavior. If you don't address that negative behavior—and, most of all, the reasons behind it—they move to the "revenge" stage, where they want to get even. If that doesn't get your attention, they proceed to the "display of inadequacy" stage, where they stop caring and interacting. Frankly, they give up.

Ninety-nine percent of the thousands of kids I've dealt with over all my years as a practicing psychologist have exhibited the first two goals of misbehavior: attention and power. These are typical behaviors that most parents see with their children—ones that can be handled by the principles of this book, including changing how you respond to your children in order to get a different outcome from them.

Kids who step beyond the power stage to the stages of revenge and display of inadequacy can also be helped by these principles, but you will need assistance beyond what this book can give. To turn those stages around, you will require professional help, including from your medical doctor, who after a checkup will likely refer you to a practicing psychologist or psychiatrist, depending on your situation.

So in this chapter, I'll briefly explain the four goals, based on concepts from Dinkmeyer and McKay, to give you an idea of which stage your child may be in. The following two chapters will delve more deeply into the two most common stages: attention and power.

Goal #1: Attention

Every child craves his parents' attention. But the attention getter's motto is, "I only count when others notice me and serve me."

It's easy to spot these kids. He's the toddler tugging on his mom's pant leg when she's talking to another mom. She's the first-grader who won't let her dad talk on the phone without interrupting him to ask a question. She's the fourth-grader hopping up and down with her hand in the air, yelling, "Pick me!" at recess.

He's the middle-schooler who gets the teacher lecture: "Now, Jared, we've talked about this before. You can't do that in class." But he does it anyway because he knows that's how he gets her attention. He's the high-schooler who is overly zealous with his peers, inserting himself in situations where he doesn't belong because somewhere along the way, he's missed developing social cues.

> "I only count when others notice me and serve me."

When these kids are told to stop their actions, they might temporarily stop. But as soon as the attention is off of them, they'll start that misbehavior again or create a new misbehavior to get the spotlight back on them.

How do parents usually respond to such kids? They're annoyed. Authoritarian parents will tell them to stop that behavior—*now*. Permissive parents will remind them, "Now, honey, I'm talking to another adult, so you know you need to wait." Or they'll say something like, "If you don't interrupt me again, I'll give you a piece of candy when I'm done."

Goal #2: Power

When a child can't get attention through positive behaviors, she moves to trying to get it through power. Her mantra becomes, "I only count when I dominate and control, when others do whatever I want them to do and when I want them to do it, and when I can do whatever I want."

It's easy to spot these kids too. She's the defiant three-year-old who stomps her foot and says, "No!" He's the second-grader who looks his dad straight in the eye and says, "You're not the boss of me."

She's the seventh-grader who tells her mom, "You're so stupid." He's the ninth-grader who, when his dad tells him to stop slamming the basketball against the house when he plays in the driveway, gets up at midnight to purposefully slam the basketball against the house, waking Dad and all the neighbors with the loud smacks.

> *"I only count when I dominate and control, when others do whatever I want them to do and when I want them to do it, and when I can do whatever I want."*

Reprimand these kids and their drive for power will only intensify. They'll continue the behavior that drives you crazy . . . and they'll do it right in your face too. Why? Because they are driven to win over you. Nothing less will do. Anything you say or do only escalates the situation.

How do parents usually respond to such kids? They get angry. Their kid is challenging their authority and brazenly doing what they've been told not to do. So parents try to knock that kid down a peg to reshape their attitude. Words fly out of their mouths like, "You little brat. You're not going to get away with that." Or, "Oh yeah? Well, I can make you do it." Or, "Stop that right now. I told you not to do that. Didn't you hear what I said?"

Goal #3: Revenge

When a parent doesn't respond well to a child's goal of power, that child proceeds to the third stage: revenge. His life mantra becomes "I only count if I can hurt others like I've been hurt." By this point, he knows he really has no power, because his power moves didn't work. He didn't get the attention he was craving even through negative behaviors. He knows others don't like him; even his family doesn't like him.

Who are these kids? They're usually older, since they've needed time to progress from stage one to stage two before getting to stage three.

She's the sixth-grader who's been rejected by her peers because of her own power plays in the peer group. Now she works extra hard to make sure they can't like her. She uses all the knowledge she gained in her previous peer groups to start a social media account that reveals their secrets and photos they'd never want others to see.

"I only count if I can hurt others like I've been hurt."

He's the tenth-grader who has one goal in life—to get even with anybody who crosses him. It doesn't matter if that person is a sibling, a teacher, or even the person who dared to step in front of him in line at the coffee shop. That guy? He deserved to be slugged.

She's the junior who takes her dad's new Jeep and crashes it on purpose, because he pays more attention to that stupid car than he does her.

He's the senior in high school who tries to commit suicide, since doing so is the ultimate revenge against people who hurt you. Or he goes on a shooting spree at the local high school to pay back all his peers who didn't notice him or rejected him.

How do parents usually respond to such kids?

The more passive, permissive parents will be hurt, thinking, *How can my kid do this to me? After all the time and hard work I've spent raising her?* They'll also feel guilty. *What did I do wrong that she turned out like this? Am I really that horrible a parent?*

The authoritarian parent will think, *So that kid thinks he can do that? Get the best of me? Well, I'm going to show him a thing or two.* He'll retaliate with words and/or actions. The sledgehammer will come down so hard on that kid, he could get squashed. Problem is, because the kid already doesn't like himself and wants to be disliked by others, parental revenge only increases his goal

126

for more revenge. This creates a cycle that's hard to break unless the parent chooses to change first.

Goal #4: Display of Inadequacy

If a parent continues to fuel a child's revenge, after a while the child gets tired. None of his ways of getting attention are working, so why bother trying? He's heard more than his fill from a parental figure about how stupid and no good he is. He's also absorbed every one of those words, furthering his discouragement about life. Since he has no place to belong, he has no purpose left in life, and nobody seems to care, he adopts a new mantra: "I'm no good. Nobody thinks I'm worth anything. I can't do anything right, so why do anything at all? I give up."

What do these kids look like?

She's the seventh-grader who wears a hoodie to hide her face and walks with head down, books clasped tightly in front of her. She doesn't talk to any other kids. At night she gets high, because it's the only time she can escape her reality.

> "I'm no good. Nobody thinks I'm worth anything. I can't do anything right, so why do anything at all? I give up."

He's the tenth-grader who heads for his room every Friday night and doesn't come out until Monday morning. He's lost his appetite, and you have to coax him to eat anything. Even the favorite foods in front of his door stay untouched. The only thing he seems to care about is his music, which is moody and a bit creepy, to be honest.

She's the eleventh-grader whose grades have slipped from As and Bs to Ds and Fs, and she doesn't seem to care. Nothing you do motivates her. She only shrugs and goes on her way. Secretly she's a cutter, because pain is the only thing that is constant in her life and that she can control.

Kids in the display of inadequacy stage have been so beaten down by life and a lack of positive attention that they're passive and bland. They've been criticized so much that they no longer react to anything you say. Since there's no reason to try or improve, why bother? They do the minimum to get by because they no longer care.

They become the 21-year-olds at street corners who run away from home and hold signs saying, "Need food." They've given up on themselves. They are so discouraged they have no self-respect left. They see no hope in life. They'd rather sit and beg than attempt to get a job.

How do parents usually respond to these kids? They honestly don't know what to do with them. They've tried everything to motivate that child, but all of it has failed. They feel hopeless. Because nothing they do seems to help and they don't see any light at the end of the tunnel, they give up too.

Next Steps

After reading these brief descriptions, you likely have an idea where your child lands on the spectrum of the four goals of misbehavior. Most of them will be in stage one or stage two. Some of you will have the misfortune of having kids in stage three, where they want to hurt others, or stage four, where they want to hurt themselves.

However, I want you to know something very important: Today is a new day. The past is behind you. You can start anew from this point forward.

But transformation starts with you. So you be the adult. Take the reins. Since you know that your kid's misbehavior has everything to do with who they are and their resulting life perceptions, as well as your parenting style and your resulting words and actions, you can climb in the driver's seat to make alterations on your current road. If you've been an MIA, authoritarian, or permissive parent, you can change that. You can become a parent who is in healthy authority over your kid. You can learn how to draw him in rather than drive him away.

Remember when I talked about my naughty cocker spaniel running away with the puzzle piece so we couldn't complete the picture? Think of your child as that complex puzzle.

> *Today is a new day. The past is behind you. You can start anew from this point forward.*

He's been built piece by piece with every experience he's had and the way he's perceived those experiences. But there's one missing piece right in the middle of his puzzle. It's you.

You're the one he wants to please. You're the one he longs to have attention from. You're the one he desires unconditional love from.

So don't delay. The completion of this puzzle is the most important thing you'll ever do in life.

"Look at Me"

*What an attention getter is and how to get
one to pay attention to you in the right way.*

"Look at me!" your seven-year-old son calls to you as he hangs upside down from the tree in front of your house.

"No, look at me. See how high I can jump," your nine-year-old says louder. She jumps up and smacks the tree, nearly knocking her brother down.

"Hey, quit it," your son says.

"No, you quit it," your daughter fires back.

And the sibling war is on, all for your viewing enjoyment.

Or your 12-year-old walks in, flourishing his math test with a big red B at the top. "Look, Dad! I didn't flunk this time. Isn't that awesome?" And you all celebrate because math is not this kid's forte.

Kids love attention. It's inherent in their nature from babyhood on. And they'll do nearly anything to be noticed, especially by their parents.

That's why they do all the crazy things they do, like smearing themselves with green Jell-O and running around the house screaming, "The aliens have landed!" right in the middle of your Skype call with work.

But some kids' goal for living is not only to get attention but to be the center of attention. If they can't get attention positively from you, they'll seek it negatively. After all, any attention is better than none at all.

They'll become what I call "attention getters."

I Only Count When . . .

Your baby girl starts crying. You whisk into the room. Your three-year-old is holding the baby's hand, which has two red semicircles that look like teeth marks.

"Did you bite your sister?" you say, shocked.

Your three-year-old has never showed any tendency to be mean. What happened?

A kid who's actively trying to get your attention is usually right in your face doing something annoying.

It's simple. Your three-year-old resents that new yelling thing in the house. She hates how much time you're spending with "it" and the lack of attention on her. You used to cuddle with her at night and read to her. Now all she gets is a quick tuck into bed and a "good night" before you whisk off to take care of "it."

When she'd had enough of being ignored, she did what she knew would make you come running. She chomped on her sister's hand, knowing the baby would scream. And it worked. You weren't happy, but you did come running. And you certainly gave her attention.

If you have a kid who's actively trying to get your attention, you'll know it. That's because he or she is usually right in your face doing something annoying.

It's your seven-year-old chanting, "Can we, huh? Can we, huh? Can we, huh?" like a cuckoo clock with OCD so you can't hear the 10:00 news. He won't go away until you promise to take him to the store the next day to get the latest hot athletic shoes.

Then there's your social drama queen who thinks you never pay attention to her. "Hello, am I invisible?" she says. "I'm, like, right here but nobody listens." And that's after you heard her rant for half an hour about so-and-so #1 at school who's no longer friends with so-and-so #2, because so-and-so #3 knew that some boy liked so-and-so #2 and told so-and-so #1 but not so-and-so #2. Your head was swimming as you tried to follow the chain of who was who.

Or it's your 15-year-old who complains, "Peas again? How come you always make peas? Just because Nitwit over there likes peas, why do I have to suffer?" You admit, this is the second time this week that you've made peas, but at least in between you made your 15-year-old's favorite—green beans . . . that is, if kids have favorite vegetables.

Is the phrase "Stop doing that" a well-worn part of your vocabulary? Then one or more of your kids is an attention getter.

Are you irritated by your kid's behavior? Is the phrase "Stop doing that" a well-worn part of your vocabulary? Then you don't have to guess. It's clear that one or more of your kids is an attention getter.

Problem is, when you say "Stop doing that," you're only affirming the pattern of attention getting because the misbehavior is paying off with attention. Remember, a child will only continue a pattern of behavior as long as it's beneficial to her. So when her life mantra has become "I only count when I'm the center of the attention," she can't stop. She has to keep striving for attention.

How Kids Get That Way

Firstborns and onlies are used to being the center of attention in their parents' world. That's why those birth orders have the highest possibility of becoming attention getters in the family.

For onlies, that attention usually remains and often intensifies as the child grows older. That's especially true if one parent is critical-eyed, often commenting on what the child could do better or differently. And heaven help that kid if he has two critical-eyed parents. With all that stress, he'll either turn it inward and end up with ulcers at age 22, or he'll rebel outwardly against the pressure by refusing to be and do what he knows his parents want him to.

The only child doesn't compete with siblings but often competes with his parents' careers. Just because he's an only child doesn't mean he gets more attention from his parents. Often they are at work or occupied with work.

For firstborns, their center of gravity changes when siblings come along. Those smaller humans garner more of their parents' attention.

That's when problems arise. Firstborns have to work harder to get any attention. Usually they begin by trying to jump over their parents' high bars of expectation, which means helping out with their younger sibling or striving to be the best at everything. They're already used to having the critical parental eye focused on them, but now it gets even worse.

134

When they do get attention, it's often negative: "You should keep an eye out for your little sister. She doesn't know any better, but you do." Or, "You're the role model for your brother now." But that firstborn knows she can never be perfect, so she's defeated before she starts. As hard as she tries, she can't get as much attention as she used to. Discouragement settles in.

Since all the things she used to do to get attention—such as drawing Mom a picture or bringing Dad coffee on a quiet Saturday morning—now are distant memories, she has to think of new ways to get attention. And I can guarantee her parents won't like many of those creative attention-getting ways.

> I can guarantee her parents won't like many of those creative attention-getting ways.

Middleborns are used to not having attention since they're sandwiched between the oldest, who gets attention for being the trailblazer, and the baby, who gets attention because he's youngest and also a born entertainer. That's why middleborns don't naturally become attention getters at home. Instead, they seek attention in social spheres outside the home, making friends far and wide. They're the one birth order that you have to go out of your way to seek out, because they're not as likely to come to you unless they really want something.

Babies of the family love attention and naturally get it since they're younger and act helpless so parents and siblings come to their rescue. Most babies don't have to work hard to get that attention because they're usually doing something loud, such as galloping like a horse down the hallway, or something crazy, such as seeing if their tongue really does stick on an icicle. Their curiosity drives them to do things like sprinkle an entire box of baking soda in the washer.

But if that baby is at the end of a long train of kids and the parents are worn down, he can feel ignored. A baby craves attention for everything he does. On the positive side, he's the sweet kid who is first to talk with Grandma on the phone and arrange birthday parties for his siblings. But if he lacks attention for doing positive things, he'll swiftly turn to antics that will force you to pay attention.

I ought to know, because I was a baby of the family who did exactly that to get attention from my parents. And because I tended to experience fewer consequences for my behavior, like many babies of the family, I continued that behavior. When I look back at all the things I did, it's a wonder my saintly mother stayed saintly. She was in the principal's office even more than I was.

A huge majority of kids today are attention getters. Ask any teacher for confirmation of that fact.

"Anthony, please don't kick Amanda's chair," a third-grade teacher says.

He looks up. "Uh, okay."

But five minutes later he's back at it again, eyeing her to see if she noticed.

Mark is the freshman class clown. "He never takes anything seriously," the vice principal tells you. "The other day, right in the middle of his English essay test, he leaped up, whooped, and started dancing down the aisle. It disturbed all the other students."

You're not surprised. That's your son, all right.

What you don't see, though, is *why* he's interrupting that class. He may not look serious, but deep inside he's discouraged. He's not good enough in anything else to stack up to the other kids, so he's got to do something that shows he's unique.

What Most Parents Do

When faced with negative attention-getting behavior, most parents tend toward extremes.

- They ignore the kid driving them crazy. It's the parental plugging of the ears and the "La-la-la-la, I can't hear you, I can't see you, you're not here."
- They lay down the law. "I told you to stop doing that, so stop. I'm not going to tell you again."
- They up the ante. "If you do that again, I'll . . ." and some threat follows.

None of those extremes help solve the *reason* for the misbehavior. It only accentuates the misbehavior because the kid is more desperate and determined to be noticed. It also heats up your own emotions, and you're more likely to lose control.

Any reaction you give encourages your child to repeat that behavior.

Any reaction you give encourages your child to repeat their behavior. If you ignore that attention-getting behavior, lay down the law, or up the ante enough, you'll have the makings of a power-driven child, which is the subject of the next chapter.

What Parents Should Do

Every March or April a childhood buddy of mine and I try to do a fishing trip together. We use tiny, barbless hooks so we're kind to the fish, and most of the time they go right back in the water unless it's a big trout that would make a great dinner.

There's one thing I learned a long time ago. If I want to catch that big, beautiful trout, I can't jerk the line. I have to play with it and bring the fish in very carefully.

You also have to fish carefully for your children's hearts to keep them in your pond and not someone else's. So what can you do if your kid is an attention getter?

Pay special attention to positive things your child does and mention them in private.

Who doesn't appreciate a compliment? It will go a long way toward healing your child's discouragement. When you talk to him in private, that's extra-special, just-for-him attention that his siblings don't get. But the attention is for *positive* behavior, not negative behavior. It will spur your child on to do more positive things since he knows you're paying attention to him for those things.

- "I appreciate the way you cleaned up the milk on the counter after you poured the cereal."
- "I saw what you did for your sister. When she was crying, you put your arm around her and said, 'It'll be okay.' That was so sweet of you."
- "It means so much to me that you remember to feed our parakeet every morning. You seem to care a lot about animals."

Every time your child does something positive, remember to smile and say, "Thank you. I really appreciate that and you."

When your child demands attention, don't immediately give it to him.

If you are on the phone when the dog and pony show starts with your child, move to another room and let him continue on his own. If he's tugging at you, demanding attention, finish what you are doing first.

Explore your child's interests with her.

When children seek attention, they're saying, "I want you in my world, and I don't spend enough time with you." So as much as that misbehavior bothers you, it's also good news. Your kid actually likes you and sees you as her number one important person.

138

When your child isn't misbehaving, comment on an interest she seems to have. For instance, "I've noticed how much time you spend in our backyard. You seem to find a lot of interesting bugs and leaves. The next time you find one, I'd love to see it."

Showing interest in your child's world also derails her from the quest for negative attention. When she's focused on finding bugs and leaves in the backyard, she won't pinch her brother, fight with her sister, or try to draw you in.

Highlight your child's uniqueness in your family and encourage her to contribute.

Kids who are feeling lost in the shuffle won't scramble as much for attention if you naturally give it to them. Think about each of your kids. What contributions can they uniquely make to your family?

Perhaps your 12-year-old is a budding creative cook. Why not ask her to make a snack for your family? In the process she gets to bask in the light of your positive attention. She's thinking, *Hey, Mom noticed I like to be in the kitchen. Maybe I can try making some brownies with mint frosting. Everybody in the family likes chocolate and mint.*

Before long, she'll be so busy thinking up recipes she won't have time for negative antics. And when she makes something good, even those siblings of hers might compliment her. That would help family dynamics all around.

The best antidote to attention-getting behavior is giving positive attention.

Rewind

Let's look at those three situations from earlier in the chapter and replay them with a positive-attention response.

The Seven-Year-Old Cuckoo Clock

Your seven-year-old chants, "Can we, huh? Can we, huh? Can we, huh?" like a cuckoo clock with OCD so you can't hear the 10:00 news. He won't go away until you promise to take him to the store the next day to get the latest hot athletic shoes.

Your response: Your eyes don't move from the news, as hard as that is. When a commercial comes on, you turn toward him and say, "No, we can't go tomorrow."

"Why?"

If you could keep track of how many times that kid said, "Why?" you'd be as brilliant as Albert Einstein or Stephen Hawking.

"We might have been able to go tomorrow, but you chose to interrupt me when you are supposed to be in bed."

"But Dad . . ."

"Now if you ask me kindly in a day or two, when I'm not busy, I might have a different response. Good night." And you go back to your TV watching.

That response might sound negative at first. It was too hard to ignore his cuckoo-clock behavior, so you chose to wait and address it during the commercial. He didn't receive a reward for his negative behavior. There would be no trip to the store. But you introduced the concept that asking nicely and during an appropriate time would garner a different response.

Good job in retraining that kid.

The Social Drama Queen

Your social drama queen claims you never pay attention to her. "Hello, am I invisible?" she says. "I'm, like, right here but nobody listens." And that's after you heard her rant for half an hour about so-and-so #1 at school who's no longer friends with so-and-so #2, because so-and-so #3 knew that some boy liked so-and-so #2 and told so-and-so #1 but not so-and-so #2.

Your head was swimming as you tried to follow the chain of who was who.

Your response: "Hmm, that's funny. I just heard you say . . .," and you repeat back to her the muddy conversation that you thought you heard for the past half hour. As you ramble on, she starts to look confused.

You don't address her snotty "invisible" comments. You don't throw back in her face, "Young lady, what do you mean I wasn't listening? I've been listening to you for a whole half hour." Instead, you snow her with her own words, then walk away, leaving her stunned since you didn't give her a chance to interject.

Later, you pick one thing out of her long blathery session to comment on: "Earlier you mentioned how bad you felt for your friend when she didn't know a boy liked her. You were embarrassed on her behalf. That shows you have a kind heart. I saw it that time the other girls were picking on the new girl in your class, and you invited her to come to our house after school. . . ."

You've refocused her negative behavior in a positive direction—on someone other than herself. Every hormone-group member needs a good dose of that.

The 15-Year-Old Pea Hater

Your 15-year-old complains, "Peas again? How come you always make peas? Just because Nitwit over there likes peas, why do I have to suffer?" You admit, this is the second time this week that you've made peas, but at least in between you made your 15-year-old's favorite—green beans.

Your response: "Ah, I guess you're right. We did have peas twice this week."

It's a simple, straightforward statement that ignores his "Nitwit" and "suffer" comments. You go back to your dinner. "Mmm, good."

You don't give your kid what he's fishing for—a family fight. His efforts fall as flat as those smushed peas on his dinner plate.

Later, you notice that he's downstairs working out, and that he's starting to get what look like muscles. "I'm impressed. What you're doing takes a lot of discipline, and you've been doing it every night for two weeks. You also seem to be researching different diets to build more muscles. I'd like to hear more about that when you're ready to tell me."

You don't give your kid what he's fishing for—a family fight.

You start to walk away, then turn back. "If you find a good vegetable other than peas and green beans, let me know. Maybe we can have that for dinner next week."

And that's the way you do it. A sense of humor goes a long way in parenting. So does appreciating your kids for who they are, highlighting the positive things they do, and encouraging them in their interests.

One of the best things you can say to a kid is, "You worked so hard on that. That has to feel good."

This type of comment hits four bases: it grants them positive attention, boosts their self-worth, starts to transform their life theme of "I only count when . . . ," *and* grows your relationship with your child.

Now that's a home run.

"There's a New Sheriff in Town"

*What a power-driven child is and how to turn
that drive for power in a positive direction.*

"I have three teenagers," Jana, an exhausted mom, told me. "One treats me like I'm on earth to serve her. I simply can't do enough for her to make her happy. Another kid I tiptoe around, afraid to set off her mood swings because they're like hurricanes descending on the house. My son's so mouthy and sarcastic, I can hardly stand him. Our living room is ground zero. I'm sick of the yelling and slamming doors. I really need some help."

What Jana needed was a solo vacation on Maui . . . and a game plan that trumped her teens. She had three power-driven kids, and they had the upper hand. They knew her hot buttons and how to push them. But as I helped her understand why her kids did what they did and how to form an easy game plan of her own, she realized she didn't have to fall for their secret strategies.

Neither do you.

Your powerful kids can work you 24/7 if you let them. All that fighting in your living room? It's to get you needlessly involved in their war.

Remember that all social behavior serves a purpose. If there isn't a payoff, kids won't do what they do. For power-driven kids, their purposive behavior results from their subconscious life mantra: "I only count in life when I'm in control and other people do what I want, when I want."

Jana was wearing herself out trying to keep up with all her kids' demands. Some of you can relate, which is why you're reading this book. Whether toddlers or teenagers, power-driven kids can indeed be exhausting.

Where Power-Driven Kids Come From

Power-driven teens aren't created out of thin air. They're taught to be powerful by someone in their house. Could that person be you?

When your kids don't act the way you want them to, do you feel that "urge" to show them who's boss? If so, you tend toward the *authoritarian* model of parenting: "I know best and you better do exactly what I say, when I say." You've done a good job showing those kids how power works and teaching them to be powerful.

Whenever I meet a power-driven kid, I know there's a power-driven parent in the house . . . or maybe two. Like two male goats, they'll butt heads in springtime and every other time.

If you, like Jana, want your kids to be happy and you tiptoe around their moods, you're a *permissive*, "whatever you want, dear" parent.

Both extremes are problematic. The *authoritarian* parent makes decisions for their child, prompting inner or outer rebellion and a lack of problem-solving skills. The *permissive* parent doesn't allow their teen to experience the results of their actions.

But if you're in healthy authority over your kid, you're going to be smarter, aren't you? In order to rear a balanced adult who doesn't think only about himself but is kind and caring toward others, there are a few things you must do:

- Allow your child to make age-appropriate decisions so he learns how to make decisions.
- Establish boundaries to keep her safe, but don't coddle her.
- Allow him to experience the consequences of real life instead of living in a fantasy world.
- Provide opportunities for her to become responsible.
- Listen to her and support her, but never do for her what she should do for herself.
- Allow him to make wrong decisions and experience the negative consequences within the loving confines of your home.

The "I know best" and the "whatever you want, dear" parenting styles don't produce a healthy child. They produce momentarily happy children who get their way when they use their power to manipulate others, but produce very unhappy, unhealthy children who can't cope in the real world when things don't go their way.

Kids who say by their behavior, "I only count in life when I'm noticed and others pay attention to me," become discouraged and proceed to this next stage of power. Their mantra becomes "I only count in life when I win, control, and dominate others." They are the kids who:

- throw you a bone when they need to get you off their case
- stare you defiantly in the eye, then head out the door to that party you've said no to

- manipulate you with tears in their baby blues so you do their bidding
- act helpless so you do what they should be doing (their chores, their homework, feeding their pet lizard)

And no, those last two in the list weren't a mistake. Surprised? Let me explain why.

Powerful Kids Come in All Different Sizes and Packages

Arlene was only five when her parents brought her to my office. She hid behind the safety of her mom's leg, peeking out at me. It wasn't until her father pried her away from her mother and plopped her like a packaged fish on a chair that I actually got to see what she looked like.

To get anywhere with her, I had to kindly suggest that the parents stay outside.

The more Arlene and I talked, the less audible her voice became. I found myself leaning closer and closer to hear what she was saying. Before long, I was on the edge of my chair.

Then it hit me. I am a psychologist, after all. That little girl had me wrapped around her finger.

Finally I said to her, "Are you trying to get me on the floor?"

"Yeah," she said with a smile.

I call that the "recognition reflex," or disclosing the goal of the child's behavior.

Arlene was a power-driven kid if I've ever seen one. And her parents, who both had master's degrees, had no idea. They'd spent half an hour explaining to me what a "sensitive" child she was and how they had to be careful around her. They were worried because she hadn't adjusted well to preschool and wasn't adjusting at all to kindergarten.

It's easy to spot the loud power-driven kids. It's because they're
. . . well, loud. But power-driven kids also come in packages that
you might not think of as powerful.

What those parents thought of as sensitivity and shyness was
power. Arlene's parents were either at work or traveling a lot, so
she'd spent a great deal of time with a live-in nanny. When her parents were home, after an initial hug
they didn't pay much attention to her.

She'd discovered early on that "be-
having badly," as her parents called it,
didn't get her anywhere except to her
room, which meant further isolation
from them. With such a lack of attention, she had plenty of time to figure
out how to manipulate them.

> It's easy to spot the loud power-driven kids. It's because they're . . . well, loud. But power-driven kids also come in packages that you might not think of as powerful.

*Oh, so they worry if I get quiet and
act sad. I know how to work that one.*

*Dad hates it if I cry. He gives me
presents.*

*If I act shy, Mom will thank people for me so I don't have to
do it.*

If I act like I'm scared, they won't make me go to school.

*All I have to say is, "Mommy, I love you. Stay with me," and
she'll stay home from work.*

Arlene had her parents figured out, and she was milking that
discovery for all it was worth. She'd rapidly progressed from an
attention-getting child to a power-driven child. But because she
wasn't loud, throwing tantrums, or screaming, her parents as-
sumed there was something psychologically wrong with her.

Obnoxious, mouthy, "princess/prince syndrome" kids are easy
to pick out as powerful. Their behavior essentially drives parents
up a wall and gets them not only to pay attention but to do exactly what their kids want them to do. But the quieter ones who

What I'd Do If . . .

Little Meadow is sitting at the Thanksgiving table. She can't find anything to say about the food except, "That looks yucky. I don't want that. That's gross."

It's a well-worn litany by now. The kid constantly complains about the food. Nothing ever pleases her.

So what do you as her parent do? You've tried telling her, "Eat it. It's good for you. You'll grow to be as big as your 135-pound father." You've also elaborated on the people in Bangladesh who would love to have that food. But neither of those statements means a hill of beans to that kid, nor would they convince her otherwise of her opinion.

There's nothing wrong with having an opinion. But there's a right way and a right time to voice it. If you're serious about turning this misbehavior around, you'll do one of three things:

1. Excuse her from the dinner table. Tell her to come back when she has written down 10 specific things she's thankful for this Thanksgiving.
2. Send her to her room for a set period of time (say, half an hour). When she comes back to the table, most of the food will be consumed and dinner will be almost over, but she can still join the family meal in progress.
3. If you have a little Judge Judy in you, ban her from the entire Thanksgiving dinner, including the pumpkin pie with the real whipped cream on top that you know is her favorite. If the guilties start gnawing at you, remind yourself of what your mother says: "Aren't leftovers great?" Little Meadow will get a taste of today . . . tomorrow.

The bottom line? Don't cooperate with your child in the fight.

You can't *make* a child eat. But you can set up circumstances where eating without complaint is a good choice on the child's part. Or you could do what most parents do: tell her to settle down, tell her she is going to eat her food, and get ready for the whining, fussing, and downhill spiral at the dinner table that will continue the battle from now until next Thanksgiving.

Now which would you rather do?

control the house's atmosphere with their moods, their tears, and the crook of their fingers are just as power driven.

How to Act When They Act Up

Though it seems contrary to how they act, powerful kids need boundaries or home won't feel safe. Your authority must be balanced and loving yet aimed toward their long-term well-being. How can you best parent power-driven kids when they act up? Here are four key strategies.

Hold them accountable.

Your son is late to school for the third time in two weeks. You've rescued him with white lies on notes before, but this time you tell the truth: "He's late because he slept in. Do whatever you do to kids who are late."

Yes, he's angry at you and embarrassed because he gets detention, but your refusal to bail him out of the mess he created is a long-term gift, showing him that his actions matter. Let him off the hook now and his purposive behavior of irresponsibility will continue.

Don't back down.

Your son's snarky remarks are way over the top at breakfast. After school, he races home to change clothes so he can get to his wrestling meet in the next town.

You confiscate the car keys. "I don't appreciate what you said this morning or how you said it, so you're not going to your wrestling meet."

He'll try everything—pleading, yelling, a weak apology—but you don't back down.

149

Yes, it's a tough evening because he misses his meet. His coach has more than a few angry words for him via cell phone, and he knows he's going to be in deeper trouble the next day. But you know that if you give in now, his plan for control will work. He'll continue dominating your house with his disrespectful mouth.

Let reality be the teacher.

Your daughter spends the night texting, talking, and giggling with her friends instead of studying for her French test. The result is a red D. The teacher forces her to retake the test when she's supposed to be cheerleading at a basketball game after school. She's fuming about how unfair life is.

You stay mum and let reality and her friends do the talking.

Realize it takes two to tango.

Your daughters are in each other's faces over a ripped clothing item. They move their fracas into your locale. Since they're fighting to get your attention, remove yourself with a simple, "I'm sure you can work it out."

Then you turn your back, hold your head high, and sashay away.

The next time your kids pull a power play, think, *What do I normally do? What will I do differently this time?*

If you want to change their behavior, start by adjusting your own.

Power trips are no fun without an audience.

Discipline 101

What it is (and isn't), why punishment never works, and why RD is the way to roll.

Imagine for a moment that you're a sheep on a hillside. I'm your shepherd for the day. I check my iPhone and see that the weather is rapidly changing. To keep the herd safe and dry, I have to move you and all your sheep buddies from point A to point B.

I say, "Hey, sheep, listen up. For your good, we need to move from Valley A to Valley B. Let's get going. Just follow me."

What happens next?

A few of you will cross your woolly arms and say, "Nuh-uh, I'm not going. I don't feel like it."

How would you feel if I whaled you on the side with a stick to get you moving in that direction?

Yes, you may move, but you certainly wouldn't be happy about it. You'd resent me inwardly, even if you obeyed me outwardly.

Many people rear their kids that way and claim that, sooner or later, they'll fall in line.

Or what if the shepherd said, "You know, I have a suggestion. The weather is turning not-so-good, and I think we ought to move somewhere . . . if you're okay with it, I mean."

Do you think those sheep would move? Nuh-uh. They'd ignore you and go on eating grass on the hillside.

Sheep and kids wouldn't respond well in either situation.

As cute and big-eyed and soft as sheep are, they're not exactly real bright. Neither are your kids since, with all due respect, they haven't been around the block for long yet.

But let's say this scene happened where I grew up in upstate New York, along the mighty Niagara River that flows to those majestic falls out onto Lake Ontario. If those sheep were being led along the swiftly flowing waters and one fell in, what would happen to the other 99?

They'd follow, like sheep do. Especially since, as cute and big-eyed and soft as sheep are, they're not exactly real bright. Neither are your kids since, with all due respect, they haven't been around the block for long yet.

Soon all those sheep will be floundering in the current of the great Niagara. In a short while, one sheep says to another, "Hey, what's that mist down there? Do you see what I see? Or is that my imagination?"

They'll float around a bend and discover Niagara Falls, and that's the end of the sheep.

Sometimes you have to say to your kids, "Nope, you're not going to walk alongside that raging river. You're not going to that place to hang out with the other kids."

"Why?" they'll inevitably shoot your way. "Everybody else is doing it."

"Because I love you, and you're my sheep and not someone else's. *Baa* . . ."

Did you catch that important line? "You're my sheep and not someone else's." Everything that happens between you and your child creates and impacts your relationship, including how you handle misbehavior.

What Discipline Really Is and Isn't

When you think of discipline, what pops into your mind? For some of you, you grew up with the idea of discipline as punishment, most often in the form of something painful inflicted on your backside or the threat of grounding.

Punishment, though, never works. What you *think* about your child's misbehavior is critically important. If you think of his behavior as "bad" and label him as "bad" for acting the way he does, there will only be one thing on your mind: retaliation and revenge.

How could he treat me like that? I'm his mother.

This kid needs to learn a lesson. How can I hammer him into submission so he'll never do that again?

Oh, so you wanna play that way, do you? Well, what you give to me, I'll give back to you and then some. Watch me.

Punishment is often exacted too quickly—on the fly or in the heat of the moment. It is a gut reaction instead of a planned response. Often the punishment far outweighs the crime.

Have you ever punished your kid with grounding for a week? How long did that last? A day? A few hours, until the kid being at home all the time drove you crazy?

You see, kids know when we can't follow through on our threats. They simply wait for us to simmer down and lay low somewhere. But do they learn anything?

Well, yes, they do. They learn how to manipulate us even more because now they know we'll fly off the handle and won't follow through on our threats.

Instead, what if you thought of misbehavior as simply behavior that's going in the wrong direction and needs an about-face for the child's good?

What if you thought of misbehavior as simply behavior that's going in the wrong direction and needs an about-face for the child's good?

If you think of that as the definition of misbehavior, you'll be less heated and reactive in the moment. You'll count to 10 before you open your mouth and insert your foot. You'll wait for an appropriate moment before you say quietly, "I don't appreciate what you did. We need to talk about this after dinner. I'll come to your room at 7:00 to discuss it."

This is a far cry from blurting out, "How could you do that? What an idiot. We'll talk about this later, and then you'll really get it." You give a timeline and give yourself a bit of space to think through a plan that's workable, not a pie-in-the-sky invention you can't make good on.

Punishment says, "If you don't do this right now, I'm gonna make you pay, and pay big." In contrast, discipline is a thoughtful plan of action intended not to inflict pain but to shape a child's future with his long-term good in mind (as well as the rest of the planet's). The follow-up action fits and doesn't exceed the crime. It puts the ownership of the misbehavior exactly where it belongs—in the offender's court.

You don't steal that ball of misbehavior and travel illegally with it to your side of the court. You don't try to make amends on your child's behalf so he's not embarrassed, inconvenienced, or uncomfortable. Sometimes kids need to be uncomfortable in order to change.

You also don't slam-dunk the ball on your kid's head for that misbehavior. You don't hammer him into the ground until he has to stop that behavior and obey.

If you use punishment as a technique in parenting and you've experienced any abuse in your past, there's an even greater risk that you might fly out of control and step outside safe boundaries in dealing with your kids. That's why it's critical to use discipline rather than punishment. Keeping control of your emotions and dealing with the issue in a straightforward manner are critical.

Discipline is a thoughtful plan of action intended not to inflict pain but to shape a child's future with his long-term good in mind (as well as the rest of the planet's).

Simply stated, punishment is something you do *to* the child. Discipline is something you do yourself on the child's behalf.

Do You React or Respond?

If you're taking a medication and you start reacting to it, that's bad. If you respond to it, that's good.

There's a huge difference between *reacting* and *responding* in parenting. When you *react*, you act in the heat of the moment, without engaging your brain first. You do what comes naturally, which nine times out of ten isn't the best action for you or your kid.

You lambaste him with:

- "You are so incredibly stupid. I can't believe you're a Smith."
- "I should have known better than to trust you."

- "Your brother never would have done that."
- "If you give me more of your lip, I'll . . ."
- "Sorry doesn't cut it. If you do that again . . ."
- "Can't you get anything right? Just once?"
- "Miss one more family dinner and I'll disown you."

Reactions are filled with insults, which later you'll feel guilty about, and threats, which you'll never make good on. The ugly interactions and aftermath tear down your relationship with your child, who thinks, *If you believe I'm an idiot, you want to disown me, and you don't trust me, why should I even try?*

After the event, the guilt you feel for losing control drives you to do all sorts of dumb things, like buy your child presents to try to win back his affection, or make promises you'll never keep, such as, "I'm so sorry. That was over the top. I'll never say anything like that again." Yet you do, even a day or so later.

Opening your mouth to insert your foot is never a productive process.

Reactions will provoke attention-starved children to move to stage two, becoming power-driven children who *make* you pay attention. Then if you still don't give them the attention they crave—which is loving them enough to discipline them rather than punish them—they move to stage three, where they are past caring what you think or say. All they want is revenge and seek to retaliate against you and every other person in the world they feel has hurt, belittled, or ignored them.

But when you *respond* to your child's misbehavior, you step back from the heat of the moment and count to 10 before you say or do anything. In those few seconds, you breathe deeply and allow your brain to engage.

We all want a good education for our kids. Remember, children will role-model what they see. What are you teaching your kids?

Are you doing what your parents did? Are you proactively living a disciplined life? Kids watch and learn from you.

Some "experts" these days advise getting in touch with and following your feelings. That's terrible advice. If you and I followed our feelings for 30 days, we'd be cellmates in the county jail.

Someone cuts you off on the freeway; follow your feelings and ram them from behind. Someone of the opposite sex looks good to you; run up and hug them.

You can't live a life like that.

Instead, take those precious 10 seconds to think, *What did I use to do in this situation? X, X, and X. Was that helpful? No. So what should I do differently this time?*

That's a far better way to live.

It also keeps the focus on the event instead of pivoting the focus to the person. Even if you don't like your child's misbehavior, you should never denigrate the child. Do you like to be called "stupid" or "idiot" or anything remotely close to that? Well, neither does your child.

What Is Reality Discipline?

Reality discipline focuses the attention on the misbehavior, not the child, and offers real-life consequences for that behavior. The person disciplining stays in control. He doesn't issue threats. She doesn't excuse the behavior. Instead, reality discipline puts the responsibility for the action squarely where it should be—in the corner of the actor (which in this case is your child).

How does it work?

Your 12-year-old is a smart-mouth, but even he outdid himself on this Saturday morning. You're a single mom who already has it tough, and that kid had the gall to say to you, "I hate your guts. You are so stupid. You never understand anything."

Can you relate? If you can't, you've never had a 12-year-old. Your time is coming, trust me.

At that moment, you don't say anything as he storms off. As one mom told me, "I retreat in my mind to a green summer field with beautiful daisies and pretend I'm picking them for a few minutes as my anger subsides."

Reality discipline focuses the attention on the misbehavior, not the child, and offers real-life consequences for that behavior.

You bide your time. Your teachable moment comes later that afternoon, when he's got a 2:00 soccer game.

At 1:30 he says, "Come on, Mom, we gotta go."

You look at him with a deadpan expression. "Go where?"

His eyes widen. "Mom. Hello, I have a game. I'm the goalie. We gotta go. Come on."

"You're not going anywhere," you say in an even tone.

"Mom! What's wrong with you? Don't you know what time it is?"

"I think you know what's wrong."

He rolls his eyes. "Oh, you're mad about this morning, aren't you?"

You shrug. "I'm not sure *mad* is the right word. Perhaps *disappointed* is."

That son of yours mentally scrambles for what to say and hits on what he thinks are the magic words. "I'm sorry, Mom."

"I appreciate you saying you're sorry. Thank you. I forgive you."

He smiles. *Ah, that was easy,* he thinks. *Got everything resolved. So she likes those words, huh? I'll store them for future use.* "Great! Then come on, let's go. I'll be late for the game."

What do you say then? "No." You stick to the decision you've already made that he's going to miss that game today.

158

Is it hard to stick to your guns? You bet. You're also thinking about the other kids who will pay for it if their goalie is missing, and the parents who will give you grief for not bringing your child to the game. Worse, your son's baby blues, the eyes that looked so lovingly at you when he was younger, are now regarding you with disbelief and betrayal.

Still, if you back down now, you'll lose everything you're working for.

"No, you're not going anywhere today."

"But Mom, I said I was sorry."

"And I forgave you. But you're still not going anywhere today."

> *If you back down now, you'll lose everything you're working for.*

Your son will try to argue with you, stomp away, and then come back to plead. When even pleading doesn't work, he'll turn on the waterworks in those baby blues.

But you still stick to your decision, Mom. Back down now, and guess who you are putting in the driver's seat of your family car? You got it, that 12-year-old. His misbehavior of disrespect won't stop. He will only remember that, after dissing you, all he needs to do is come to you to say, "I'm sorry." Then he can go on his merry way to his activity.

Would he learn anything, though? Except how to effectively manipulate his mother?

Reality discipline puts the responsibility where it should be. After all, that's the way life works, isn't it? Don't do your homework and the teacher gives you a big fat F. Don't do your work at your job and you'll get reprimanded or fired. Betray a friend and he's not likely to circle back around to befriend you again. Nobody in those situations is going to give you a second chance.

So, parent, let reality do the talking instead of you. Let your child experience real-life consequences instead of made-up fantasyland ones.

Believe me, when your son's soccer friends give him the what-for because he didn't show and he has to scramble to figure out what to say, he's going to be embarrassed enough not to want to do it again. If the other parents ask you where you were, tell them honestly. "I didn't appreciate my son's disrespectful mouth in the morning, so I kept him home."

Sure, some die-hard soccer parents may give you grief, but then again, they're the ones embarrassing their kids anyway by yelling at them on the field, "What's wrong with you? Why didn't you make that goal?" But the majority of parents will be looking at you with awe. *Wow, if only I had the guts to do that.*

Reality discipline puts the responsibility where it should be. After all, that's the way life works, isn't it?

For you, it's a win-win all around: a more respectful kid who knows he can't get away with murder, and a respectful peer group that admires you. But most important, you're establishing your authority over your child in a healthy way. There is no emotional haranguing and no punishment. You aren't reacting to the situation and your "bad" child. Instead, you are proactively taking the reins to discourage the situation from happening again.

Simply stated, you're holding your child accountable for his mouth. After all, you are responsible for your own mouth, aren't you? Then why shouldn't he be?

Reality discipline has everything to do with developing your relationship with your child. Punishment tears down that relationship; discipline builds it up.

When you hold your child accountable for his behavior and allow him to experience real-life consequences for it, he grows into the type of healthy adult you'd like him to be:

- respectful of you and other authority figures
- caring and kind to those less fortunate
- considerate of others and their belongings
- healthy in self-worth but not self-centered
- resilient in tough times and unafraid of failure
- a hard worker, open to feedback about how to do his job better

That is, after all, what you're aiming for—a balanced, healthy adult—right?

Setting Boundaries That Work

Parents ask me all the time about whether or not they should have rules for their kids. Children feel safest with boundaries set so they know what to expect. Some rules are no-brainers and necessary, like "Thou shalt not cross the street when a car is driving past at light speed." But children work best with guidelines that they help set themselves—age-appropriately, of course. It's a bit harder to rebel against your own rules.

If you gathered your kids and asked them, "What rules do you think we should have in this house?" some of their first answers would be silly: "We get to eat cookies for breakfast every day" and "The person who forgets to put the toilet seat down gets a swirly." But when they get more serious, their answers will be far more stringent than the guidelines you might come up with:

- "Anyone who fights has to do the dishes for a month."
- "If you do something bad, you have to write 'I'm sorry' a hundred times."
- "If you yell at someone else, you have to eat a raw onion."
- "If you forget to do a chore, you have to do two dozen chores the next week."

See what I mean? Of course, it's more fun to come up with ideas to discipline others than it is to be the recipient of that discipline. Then the thrill fades quickly, especially if you're the one to be treated to a swirly. But as your kids grow older, it's even more important to let them be in the driver's seat of their own discipline. After all, how will they learn about holding themselves accountable if you rule the roost and tell them what to do?

So I did my best to hold all five of my kids accountable. Here's one example.

When my daughter Krissy was a teenager and had the family car at an out-of-town football game, she phoned to ask, "Dad, what time do I need to be home?"

"Honey, you know what time," I said. "Be home at a reasonable hour."

"But Dad, what time do I need to be home? I'm at the pizza place, and the team isn't even here yet."

"Then you don't want to come home yet, do you?"

"No, and that's why I'm calling you. What time do I need to be home?"

Again I said, "Just be home at a reasonable hour."

"Okay," she said with some annoyance. Then there was the click of the phone.

Forty minutes later, she woke me up for the second time. It was now 10 minutes after midnight. "Dad, this is Krissy."

I never would have guessed.

"What time do I need to be home?"

"Be home at a reasonable hour," I mumbled, half asleep.

"Dad, would you just tell me what time I need to be home?"

I could hear the flailing of her arms on the other side of the phone.

"Krissy, you're 16 years old, you've got good brains in your head, and you've got the family car. Just be home at a reasonable hour."

"Okay." *Click.*

Seven Top Principles of Reality Discipline

1. Realize that your goal is to be in healthy authority over your children.
2. Hold children accountable for their actions.
3. Watch for the teachable moments.
4. Let reality be the teacher.
5. Use actions, not just words, and stick to your guns.
6. Pick your battles carefully.
7. Remember that relationships come before rules.

Thirty-five minutes later—and you as a parent know this feeling of not being able to truly fall asleep until all your kids are in the nest—I was still awake. I heard the garage door open. Footsteps came in the door. I looked at my bedside clock. It was 12:45.

I smiled. Krissy had booked it home right after I'd told her she had good brains in her head. Her actions proved her good decision-making skills and that she was dependable with the family car.

It's easy to say to a kid, "Here are the rules." It's more difficult to say, "I trust you, I believe in you, and you have good judgment. I'll be right here in your corner, cheering for you."

Some of you are already thinking, *Good for you that you have a responsible kid. If I told my son that, he'd never come home.*

Then a good dose of reality discipline should follow. That kid wouldn't go out the door with the family car again anytime soon.

So here's my suggestion. Believe the best and you'll get the best . . . most of the time. But don't be surprised when your kids are kids and they misbehave. Then look for the teachable moment—like not giving him the car keys when he wants to go to the mall a week later—and let reality do the talking instead of you.

Enough said?

Want Your Child to Succeed?

If you want the best out of your child, let him fail.

What? you're saying. *Did I read that right?*

Well, let me ask you a few questions:

- Do you yell, threaten, or cajole your child to do simple, routine things like get up for school, get dressed, eat, do homework, or perform a chore?
- Are you overly involved, smoothing your child's path in life?
- Do you complete school assignments that seem too difficult for your child or make excuses if she doesn't finish them on time?
- Do you worry if your child doesn't seem happy?

Let me be blunt. An unhappy child is a healthy child, and failure is a step on the road to success. Look at it this way: If you're happy and everything is going well, are you motivated to change? No. It's when things *aren't* going well that you start thinking, *Hmm, that didn't work so well. Maybe I should try something different next time.*

The same thinking is true for your child. When a child is unhappy, it's often because he's done something wrong or failed to do something he should have done, or simply because you, parent, aren't falling in line with his wishes at this instant. If so, being unhappy will motivate him to do something different next time.

Feeling good is temporary, and emotions change from moment to moment. True self-worth is established when a child works hard for something, earns that something, and can call it his own: *I did that myself. Wow.*

Sometimes a child will struggle and work hard, yet the outcome isn't good. Still, in that situation he learns something—what doesn't work—and he can do things differently next time.

But how your child proceeds—and what he does or doesn't get away with—is largely up to you. When your child is struggling, ask yourself, *Is this something he is capable of doing on his own if he works hard?* If so, let him struggle, work hard, and potentially fail too. When a child pulls his weight and learns responsibility and accountability for his actions, he establishes a healthy self-worth, which is based on three ABCs: acceptance, belonging, and competence.

Acceptance

Your kid craves your approval and will live up to your expectations for her. Not allowing her to do things on her own is telling her, "You're the dumbest kid I've ever seen" and "I don't think you can do it by yourself, so I have to help." But with your approving nod and attitude of "Go for it! I know you can do it," your kid will fly high and keep going for a long time on that kind of wind.

Belonging

Everybody needs to belong somewhere. Will it be in your home, where it's okay to try and fail, or in your kids' peer group, where false information flourishes and values can be very different? Are your kids secure in belonging to you? They'll never truly feel like a part of your family unless they contribute.

Competence

Want your kids to gain psychological muscles to power through whatever comes their way in life? Give them responsibility. When they follow through—whether it's feeding the dog or cleaning the kitchen—say, "Good job. Bet that made you feel good inside." Properly used, that temporary "feel good" can inspire kids to do it again.

When they fail to follow through, don't do the task for them. A hungry dog waking your daughter up at 1:00 a.m. or you not being able to make dinner because the kitchen's a mess ought to do the trick without any vocal output on your part.

When your kids fail, they learn what *not* to do the next time around. Like you do.

Your child is much smarter and more capable than you think. Sometimes she's just workin' ya. So, for her sake and for yours, don't fall for it.

Keeping a Long-Term Perspective

One last caveat: Only use discipline when it counts. That means you pick your battles carefully or you can run the risk of overdoing it. You won't like every one of your child's behaviors. But not every misbehavior is a hill to die on.

Does it honestly matter if your teenager dyes her hair blue? The dye will eventually fade, or she'll figure out that the new color doesn't go with her current wardrobe.

If your four-year-old has to line up all her stuffed animals before bedtime and it takes her an hour, but she pitches a fit if you try to hurry her up, then tell her an hour earlier that it's time to be heading to bed. That will give her the time to nest that she wants (make sure it's without you and she doesn't pull you into her organizing world), and she'll get to bed on time.

If your eight-year-old never cleans his room, leave it be. He'll get around to cleaning it when he can't find his baseball glove.

If your 11-year-old son drinks out of the milk jug and that drives you crazy, buy two gallons of milk instead of one. Mark his with his name in bold black letters. It'll keep you from running to the store as often since he drinks a quart with every bowl of cereal, and the rest of the family will be happier that he doesn't drain *their* gallon of milk.

You see, we parents often major on minors, the little annoyances that drive us bonkers. Instead, let reality do the talking. That 16-year-old son who insists on multiple ear piercings and a nose ring will soon find out that he may have a tough time getting a summer job.

When I was assistant dean of students at the University of Arizona, I chuckled at the transitions in students' appearances from freshman orientation through senior year. At freshman orientation, a boy was usually decked out in Mom-approved wear—fresh haircut, clean khakis, and so on. Within a month or so after Mama was out the door, that boy started to look scruffy and unshaven, and those khakis were crumpled or replaced with ripped jeans. Sometimes an earring or two was added, as well as a more rebellious attitude. By senior year, though, that boy was back to Mom-approved wear, sans earrings because he had to go to job interviews.

We parents often major on minors, the little annoyances that drive us bonkers. Instead, let reality do the talking.

If you're the parent of a teenager, have patience and ride out the wave. Your alien will return to looking like your child sooner or later.

Trends come and go. Keep the focus on your relationship and you'll never be out of style or go wrong.

Time-Tested Strategies That Really Work

Practice may not make perfect, but
it leads to behavioral change.

My sister makes this incredible fresh raspberry pie. She's spent years perfecting it, and my family has enjoyed sampling it. The crust is so flaky that it melts in your mouth like a soft croissant. Even writing about it now makes my mouth water.

But one time, when my sister walked through my door with that fresh raspberry pie, she dropped it right on the kitchen floor. The pie launched its deliciousness in multiple directions.

Sande, our kids, and I took one look and grabbed spoons from the drawer. We scooped those pie remnants right up off the floor and ate them.

Sometimes life isn't perfect. You have to take what you can get.

You may not have been the world's best parent up to this point. Perhaps you've been busy with your career, embroiled in a divorce, or battling your own issues as a result of your prior experiences. Your kids have fallen through the cracks of your own needs.

Maybe it bothered you when I talked about the importance of imprinting early on in a child's life. You missed your kid's early years because you worked long hours. Or you might have fallen into the activity trap of farming your kid out to other people—sports coaches, ballet classes—so they'd be "competitive" and wouldn't miss out on anything in their future.

Perhaps you've gone the route of an authoritarian, calling the shots for your kid. You had no idea that your own behavior could provoke his misbehavior. Or you erred on the side of permissiveness, never allowing your child to make decisions, fail, or struggle. You didn't know you were doing your child a disservice by trying to help him and smoothing his path in life.

What do I do then? you wonder. *My kids are 12 and 14. Isn't it a little too late?*

The good news is that it's never too late. Change starts with you.

An apology is a good first step. "I've been thinking. As a parent I've done some things wrong up to this point. But from now on, I want you to know you're going to see a new mom [dad] around this house."

Your kids will look at you with upraised brows, thinking, *Okay, whatever.*

Until you show them that you're indeed different, they won't believe it. That's because they've been your guinea pigs for years as you've tried different strategies.

> The most difficult things are staying consistent and not giving in when you're worn down.

You need a new plan so you can make some progress. It won't be easy, especially if you've let some years go by in your parenting. But it'll be worth it. The most difficult things are staying consistent and not giving in when you're worn down.

There's an old saying that "practice makes perfect." But you don't have to be a perfect parent. You only need to be a better, wiser parent, and that takes time, patience, and commitment. This book is about not only retraining your child but also retraining yourself.

If you don't commit to doing a few things differently, you'll slip right back to your earlier behavior, and your child will continue his misbehavior.

Want Lasting Behavioral Change?

If you want lasting behavioral change, here are 10 time-tested strategies of how to get it. I know they work, because I've used them with my own five kids and shared them with countless other families I've counseled over nearly four decades.

1. Put the ball in the court where it should be.

When you hold your child accountable for his words and actions, you show respect for him. Never do anything for your child that he should do for himself.

That homework he complains about? It's his, not yours.

That bad attitude he showed that got him in trouble with the coach? He needs to own up to that and take the consequences.

> Never do anything for your child that he should do for himself.

You shouldn't make excuses for him, like, "Oh, Coach, my son just had a bad day. You've had bad days, haven't you?" You also shouldn't project blame for his behavior on yourself: *If only I was a better parent, he wouldn't be like that. It's all my fault.* No, the fault is his, and the responsibility should rest squarely on his shoulders. The sooner he learns that disrespectful language and bad attitudes aren't the way to fly, the better off he and everyone around him will be both now and in the future.

Those chores she's assigned to do? They're hers, not yours. If she doesn't do them, pay a sibling to do them out of her allowance.

Does that mean you don't help her sometimes, like when she's ill? No. After all, you appreciate it when people help you with your tasks at such times. The difference is, you don't expect or plan on that help.

It should be the same for your kids. Holding children accountable prepares them for life outside your home, where people won't go easy on them if they don't carry their workload or complete their part of the deal.

2. Look for teachable moments.

Age-appropriate moments surround you every day, when you look for them.

Your four-year-old yells, "No!" when you ask her to sit at the breakfast table. An hour later, she whines, "Mommy, I'm hungry."

What do you say? "Snack time isn't for another couple of hours. Breakfast has already passed."

"But Mommy, I'm hungry!" she insists, stomping her foot.

Age-appropriate moments surround you every day, when you look for them.

"I understand. You can have a snack in a couple of hours. The next time I ask you to come to breakfast, you may not want to say no."

At that same breakfast table your 11-year-old eyes his toaster waffle with disgust. "Again? I had this two days ago. Can't you make anything else? I'm sick of these. You might as well give me nothing. I can do it myself."

You ignore his comment, exit the kitchen, and go about your business. When you pick up his plate later, there's a ring of syrup and the toaster waffle is strangely missing.

The next morning when he shows up to eat, his plate is on the table, but there's nothing on it. He stares at it. "Where's my breakfast?"

"Oh, I'm doing what you said yesterday—giving you nothing. You said you could do it yourself, so have at it."

After that kid has to get his own breakfast—including finding the bowl, the cereal, the spoon, and the milk that's hidden behind the pickles, ketchup, and three-day-old pizza in the fridge—and still make it out the door on time, he might be slurping down those waffles tomorrow. Or he might have to set that alarm half an hour earlier to create his own breakfast. Either way, he's developing an understanding of and appreciation for what you do.

So look for those teachable moments. They'll stick for a much longer time than any lecture ever could.

3. Use reality discipline instead of punishment.

It's easy to tell kids what to do and what not to do, or to threaten them with punishment for their misbehaviors. What's harder is thinking ahead of time about a new parenting strategy so you can have a different outcome, then acting on that plan.

Real-life consequences are terrific training tools for your kids. If they face a little reality now, they'll be better off when they have to face it outside your protective doors.

Your teenage son hates to clean his room. It's been months since you've seen a glimpse of the floor. He tells you he's going to bring a friend over to do homework after school. The light in his eyes tells you it's a girl he's interested in. Knowing how curious girls are, you want to tell him to clean his room in case she takes a peek. But you don't, because you have a higher purpose in mind.

That girl does eventually wander down the hall and take a peek. Afterward she enters the kitchen wide-eyed, grabs her backpack, and says, "I gotta go."

"Now?" your son says. "But you just got here."

"It's not going to work out," she blurts out.

"But . . . why?" your son manages.

"Your room." She shudders. "Just . . . no."

And off she goes. You certainly can't blame her.

> If they face a little reality now, they'll be better off when they have to face it outside your protective doors.

A few minutes later, you hear your son's bedroom door open. You peek around the corner. He's standing there with his mouth open. "Wow, this *is* bad," he mutters.

That night he's up late, and the thumping and rearranging of his room interrupts your sleep. The next morning, he has panda eyes and drags himself out the door.

You can't stand it. As soon as he's gone, you hurry down the hall and peek in his door. Wonder of wonders, you can see floor. The pizza boxes, clothes, books, shoes, and athletic gear are no longer scattered across every available surface. It's still not your kind of clean, and the odor is locker-room musty, but you smile.

A miracle has happened in your home.

Will your son ever capture that girl again? She isn't likely to be seen again in his life after her view of that room. But the next time he brings a girl home, I bet he'll have his room spotless and even open the windows and get one of those Black Ice air fresheners.

Project complete.

Reality did the trick without you expending energy or saying one word. That's the power of reality discipline.

4. Say what you mean and mean what you say.

If you're on the expressway and the car in front of you keeps switching lanes, it can be irritating. "Why can't they pick a lane and stay in it?" you growl, since they're blocking you from speeding around them.

Not doing what you say can be just as irritating to your kids. That's why it's critical that you choose the words you use with them very carefully. Don't say anything you're going to have to back down from.

> Don't say anything you're going to have to back down from.

"You're grounded for life!" That isn't likely to happen, is it? So don't say it in the first place.

If your kids know that you say what you mean and mean what you say, it will curb a lot of their misbehaviors. Why? Because they know there are power and consistency behind your words. You aren't merely flinging them at your kids because you're momentarily upset.

After saying what you mean and meaning what you say, there's another step: following through on those consequences.

After being faced with a running-on-fumes car too many times when you have to get out the door to work, you make a family announcement: "Anyone who drives my car is responsible for making sure there is at least a quarter tank of gas in it before they park it. Otherwise, that person will lose their privileges to drive the car for a week."

A week later, you drive your car two blocks and it's out of gas. You're half an hour late to work because you have to fill up the car, and your boss isn't happy.

The last person to drive the car was your daughter, who went to the mall with her friends on Saturday. Your first inclination is to tongue-lash your daughter as soon as you get home. Instead, you bide your time for that teachable moment.

Why Your Kids Misbehave—and What to Do about It

That night she asks, "Hey, Mom, I can't find the car keys. They aren't in the kitchen."

"No," you reply. "They're not."

"I need the keys. I'm supposed to meet Kelle at Starbucks."

"You're not going anywhere tonight."

"Mom! I have to get to Starbucks! What's your problem?" your sassy daughter says.

You laugh lightly. "It's not my problem. It's your problem."

She frowns. "What do you mean?"

"Well, I was late to work this morning since the car was nearly empty. The last person who drove it was you."

"Oh, I forgot. I'll fill it up from now on."

You nod. "Thank you. I'm glad to hear you say that."

She smiles. "Great. So then, I need the car keys."

You go back to the task you were doing. "As I said, you're not going anywhere tonight."

Your daughter will test you to see if you're saying what you mean and meaning what you say, especially if you've backed down before. But this time you won't back down because you know what's at stake—your daughter's future as a responsible human being.

She won't be happy with you that night, but so what? You weren't happy when your boss unleashed his anger on you that morning.

Sometimes a child has to be unhappy to be healthy. So don't change lanes and don't back down. Far in the future your child will think back to this moment and thank you for sticking to your guns.

5. Say something once, then walk away.

You are the writer of your very own family screenplay. You're the one who taught your characters to misbehave. Now you need to change the screenplay.

Every time you tell your kids what to do, you program them to talk back and to go out of their way not to do what you said.

176

It's called "human nature," and it started way back in the days of Adam and Eve.

When I asked a kid once how he knew when to pay attention if his mom called, here's what he said: "The first time, I ignore it. She'll call again. The second time, if she's starting to get mad, she'll add my last name. But I know I still have time, because she's on a three-call system. When she adds my middle name and her voice goes up a notch—that's the third call—then I know I need to get going and do what I was supposed to do, or else I'll be in real trouble."

It's no wonder kids get Mommy-deaf or Daddy-deaf. They know exactly how long they can safely ignore us.

See how we train our kids to misbehave? It's no wonder kids get Mommy-deaf or Daddy-deaf. They know exactly how long they can safely ignore us and the steps we'll go through. In short, they've got us figured out.

So here's the new plan. You say something only once, and then you walk away.

There's no follow-up call or threat. If that task isn't done, then reality discipline follows. B doesn't happen until A is completed. That means he doesn't go to his baseball game until he's finished the task he's supposed to do, even if he doesn't arrive until the final inning.

So give your vocal cords a rest. You only need them one time, not three.

6. Remember that fighting is an act of cooperation.

You can't fight by yourself. You need someone to fight with you. It takes two to do that emotional tango. You can't do that dance if one of the partners withdraws.

You're the adult, so you're the one who needs to change first. Simply refuse to engage in the fight from now on.

"Mom, does this look good on me?" your daughter asks.

You sigh. It's starting again. You hate these battles over clothes. She asks for your opinion but then wants to fight you over it. Instead of opening your mouth, stop and think, *What did I use to say or do in this situation?*

Any time you said, "Sure, that looks fine," she asked, "Does it really? It doesn't make me look fat?"

You couldn't win no matter what you said after that, and usually tears followed.

If you said, "Your red shirt would look better with your jeans," she rebutted with, "But that shirt has [whatever] wrong with it."

Your blood pressure started to rise when she insinuated that you're old and you don't know what fashion is. It skyrocketed when she added that you're stupid. Then the fight was fully on.

So what will you do this time for a different outcome?

You'll refuse to engage in the dog and pony show. Getting in your kid's business and offering up your opinion is a perfect setup for an all-out parent-child war . . . after which that child will go back to doing what she would have done anyway. Why go there in the first place?

> *Getting in your kid's business and offering up your opinion is a perfect setup for an all-out parent-child war*

In answer to her question, you answer simply, "What matters is that you like what you're wearing."

She swivels, ready to start the fight. "What does that mean?"

"Exactly what I said," you say, and then exit.

Those previous principles of "say what you mean and mean what you say" and "say something once, then walk away" come in very handy when your child is trying to fight with you, don't they? If you don't engage, there's no fight.

End of story.

7. Decide what's worth the battle.

Parents the world over are infamous for picking fights with their kids over minor things when they should be focusing on major ones. Some things aren't worth going to war over.

Your kid dyes his hair purple and thinks it's cool. Why should you care? It's *his* hair. If his school allows this new style, then your son gets to experiment with his individuality. If the school doesn't, then reality discipline will come into play when the principal calls him in and tells him to get rid of that style.

If the purple hair stays for a while and he even adds some other colors to go with it, don't worry. Enjoy the psychedelic ride. I guarantee that by the time he takes his first job in Manhattan, he won't have purple hair.

Authoritative parents pay more attention to their child's heart than the clothes they have on or the color or style of their hair. One of my daughters has had every color in the rainbow in her hair, I think, including blue. It's no surprise that she ended up going to art and design school and has had jobs as a toy designer with large companies like Disney and Hasbro.

> *Sort out what truly are misbehaviors—which need to be corrected for the child's good—from behaviors that result from your child figuring out who he or she is.*

As you look at your child's behaviors, sort out what truly are misbehaviors—which need to be corrected for the child's good—from behaviors that result from your child figuring out who he or she is.

Jenna's room was a continual mess of art projects and homework. The beat-up Volkswagen bug she'd scraped up enough money to buy at age 16 was littered with her changes of clothes, coffee cups, a backpack, and anything else that happened to be left in there for the week. Every once in a while she'd clean it out, but not often enough for her father.

As I talked with the firstborn dad, he understood that what he saw as misbehavior on his lastborn daughter's part came from her artistic personality and her heart for people. The same girl who had that messy room and car worked a part-time job, volunteered at an elderly facility once a month, and tutored disadvantaged kids on Saturday mornings.

Yes, sometimes her grades slipped a bit too, which also drove him crazy since his parents had hammered him about grades below an A. But that girl's heart was definitely in the right place. She was courteous, kind, and generous to everyone she came in contact with. Everyone she knew loved her and admired her.

What her dad saw as Jenna's laziness in not cleaning her car or studying enough was an incorrect perception of who his daughter really was. Once he changed his thinking and followed through with action, including the words "I'm sorry," the chasm that had existed between them started to close.

Each of your children will be different. Different isn't wrong; it's just different. Jenna wasn't like her structured, perfectionistic older brother, who was in law school. She wasn't like her middle sister, who was studying music in college. She was a social, rather unorganized baby of the family who had a heart of gold for people.

So what are you paying attention to? The things about your child that drive you crazy, or your child's heart? Choose your battles wisely.

8. Don't snowplow your child's roads.

If you've rescued your kids from consequences they should have had, you're not doing them any favors. Experiencing consequences for misbehavior is what naturally nips it in the bud.

Your daughter leaves school early, saying she has to go to a doctor's appointment. The school doesn't have a note from you, so they call you to check in.

You don't want her to get in trouble, so you say, "Oh, yes, Mrs. Smith, my daughter does have an appointment. In fact, we're at that appointment right now. Thank you for checking in." Then you hang up.

When your daughter comes home, you say, "Where have you been? The school called."

> *Experiencing consequences for misbehavior is what naturally nips it in the bud.*

She waves her hand. She's used to you lying for her to get her out of any trouble she might be in. "You told her I was at the appointment, right?"

"Well, yes, I—"

She cuts you off. "So then it's all good." She brushes by you and heads to her room.

Later that day, you overhear her talking to a friend on her cell phone. "No, I didn't get in trouble. The school called Mom, and she covered for me." A laugh. "Yeah, I know. She's so stupid. She doesn't know anything."

Stop right there. Are you really going to allow that to continue? There's a fast way to halt such lying and disrespectful behavior. You tell the truth and don't cover for her.

So you call the school back. "This is Miranda's mom. There's something I need to tell you." You explain that you had no idea what your daughter was up to earlier but were afraid she'd get in trouble, so you lied. You apologize for lying and then say, "I still don't know where my daughter was, and I don't want this to happen again. So I'd appreciate it if you'd call her into the office tomorrow and talk to her about her unexcused absence."

Your daughter is going to be furious after school the next day, but she'll come to grips with the fact you're not going to lie anymore for her.

Remember that in order to change your child's misbehavior, you have to change your own first. Snowplowing your child's roads harms her now and in the future.

181

9. Don't sail into your child's wind.

Parents tell me all the time, "I just can't shut up."
Really? You can't?
You can. But you're not disciplined enough to close your mouth before you insert your foot or spark a fight. So don't tell me you can't do it. You're really saying, "I choose not to do it."

But look at the results. Carnage is strewn all over your house, and you and your child aren't talking to each other. Who made that choice for you? Was it an alien who invaded your body? No, it was you.

No one *made* you angry. You allowed yourself to become angry.

Your son directly disobeys you and you call him on it.

He gets in your face. "Dad, I'm sick of you telling me what to do. I have a life of my own, you know."

Now is the moment for you to choose. Will you step into your child's wind and allow him to control you through your own anger? If so, that action is easy. You let your instinctive reactions take over.

Choosing to respond is harder but a much better option in the long run. You have to swallow those gut reactions, count to 10 in your head, breathe deeply, and not speak until you're controlled.

Then you say, "You're welcome to your own opinions. But the fact remains that you didn't do what I asked you to do."

Your kids are highly skilled at creating the massive emotional winds that swirl through your house and loop you in. But you have a choice. You don't have to be swept up in the tumult.

10. Don't ask them questions.

We parents are so good at asking questions. We're masters, in fact.

- "Honey, how was your day?"
- "Oh, what is that?"

- "When is your astronomy project due?"
- "What did you learn today in kindergarten?"

But kids, like husbands, hate questions as much as they hate being told what to do. Being asked questions will only prompt them to shut their mouths.

Nuh-uh, I'm not saying anything, just in case it's incriminating, they're thinking. *The less Mom and Dad know, the better. I'll tell them if I have to. Otherwise they'll get in my business and try to handle it. That would be really embarrassing.*

Instead, ask for their opinion or make an open-ended statement:

- "I need to buy a new laptop since mine isn't functioning well anymore. You're so good with technology, so I'm hoping you could steer me toward some ideas. I don't need a lot of bells and whistles, but I do need a good sound card and a couple programs to create some presentations for work. Would you be able to help me research that?"
- "This year I'd like to do a family Christmas card, but we've got a limited budget. You're so creative, I was thinking maybe you could give me an idea or two."

Asking for their opinion shows that you respect them as people and value their input. It's far different than firing questions at them that put them on the defensive. Pointing out skills your kids have that can benefit the whole family is a positive way to meet their need for attention. It will redirect their energy from misbehaving into pursuing mutually beneficial activities.

I'd say that's a good deal, wouldn't you?

Practicing these time-tested strategies won't make you a perfect parent, but it'll certainly make you a better one. As you change, your kids will begin to change.

Read the sidebar "My Plan for Behavioral Change" every day for the next week or two until it becomes part of your thinking. But don't post it where your kids can see it. Simply start becoming the new mom or dad you want to be, and let them be confused and off-kilter for a while.

Let the fun begin.

My Plan for Behavioral Change

I will:

- Put the ball in the court where it should be.
- Look for teachable moments.
- Use reality discipline.
- Say what I mean and mean what I say.
- Say something once, then walk away.
- Remember that fighting is an act of cooperation.
- Decide what's worth the battle.

I won't:

- Snowplow my child's roads.
- Sail into my child's wind.
- Ask questions.

Conclusion

Transformation Guaranteed

---

*You don't have to be perfect. You don't
have to have a perfect kid. You just need
to walk the road of life together.*

Fast-forward a few years to an inevitable moment: when that child you've reared as best you can for 18 years is walking out your door and into a new phase of life. It'll come way faster than you think.

When Sande and I were anticipating taking Holly, our firstborn, to Grove City College as a freshman, I kidded my wife about what a mess she'd be saying goodbye to her once little girl. Little did I know how influential that day would be in *my* life.

We had two cars to take her and all her stuff to college. When we arrived, we saw a welcome sign: "Men this way. Women that way." We followed the women's direction and pulled up in front of the dorm, and guys in blue button-down shirts swarmed over and emptied out our cars in 30.2 seconds. I'm not kidding. It was

185

masterful. I remember eyeing those guys and wondering if one of them would mean something to my Holly someday.

Once in the room, we met the roommates and the parents of the roommates, who looked as stunned and uncomfortable as Sande and I did.

When it was obviously time for us parents to leave because we'd been through all of the "Welcome, Parents" program, I said, "Uh, we should get going."

Holly, who has never backed down from anything in her life, blurted out, "Dad, is there a ball game on or something?"

It's a family joke that I never miss a ball game, come rain, snow, or tsunami.

I shook my head. "No, there's no ball game. I just think we need to move along."

Sande chimed in, "Besides that, I haven't made Holly's bed yet."

I frowned. "You are *not* making Holly's bed. She's a college student."

My wife, the loveliest, sweetest woman on the face of the earth, gave me "the look." The look that says, "Back off, Charlie, if you know what's good for you. I *am* going to make that bed."

I'm smarter than I look, so I backed off. The bed got made.

> My wife, the loveliest, sweetest woman on the face of the earth, gave me "the look." The look that says, "Back off, Charlie, if you know what's good for you."

Then we started this process of saying goodbye. There was a huge lump in my throat. Since I don't like public emotion (I am a male, after all), I hightailed it to the car. I wanted to stay in control. I knew it was do-or-die time, and I wanted to get the deal done before I died.

Then I looked over, and Holly was hugging my wife. Sande's tears were streaming down. I'm talking big rivers of liquid.

I knew at that instant we *had* to get out of there. So I hustled to the driver's side of the car.

All of a sudden, Holly ran to me. "I love you, Daddy," she said, and threw her arms around me.

I turned to hug her and lost control. Tears started to flow.

Shocked, she said, "Daddy!" in that "holy crow, are you over-reacting" voice.

At that moment, I didn't think of the times she'd misbehaved, like when she was mad at me and told me I ought to read my own parenting books. I didn't think about the times she'd fought with her siblings, the mind games she'd played on her little sisters to keep the upper hand, or the disgusted looks she'd give us when we let Kevin II, the then baby of our family and the only boy, get away with something we'd never have let her do.

Those times didn't even cross my mind.

Instead, as stupid as this sounds, I thought of the tiny slip of a bra that I'd stepped on in the bathroom when Holly was 10 years old. Back then it was strung on the floor, so it got my attention. I lifted the thing up high in the air and examined it, and I'm telling you, I didn't have the foggiest idea what it was.

I went around the corner, still holding the item pinched between my fingers, and found my wife. "Honey, what is this?"

She swiveled, looked at the item, and put her hand over her mouth. I could tell she was trying hard not to laugh. "Oh, honey, that's Holly's bra."

I looked at it again. *My Holly's bra? This looks like it could grow up to become a bra someday.*

"It's a training bra," Sande explained.

But Holly didn't have anything to train. Even dumb-as-mud dads notice that.

It boggled my mind that as I was saying goodbye to my daughter at college, I was thinking about that incident. Now I thought, *You can't be grown-up. You're still a little kid, 10 years old, in a training bra. Before that you were shorter than a yardstick. You can't be going away to college.*

But here we were.

Finally, I said in a broken voice, "Holly, you better go."

And you know what Holly Leman did? My firstborn walked away. She didn't walk away all slumped over and dejected. She wasn't crying her eyes out. I was.

I said to my wife, "Let's get out of here." Then I swiveled toward Holly and yelled, "Holly, don't forget. Call us tonight, honey." She gave a little wave, called "Okay" over her shoulder, and continued walking. When she disappeared through the door, the weight on my heart was crushing.

The entire two-and-a-half-hour drive home was the worst drive of my life. Sande and I barely talked. We stopped partway, still stunned, and had lunch at Red Lobster. Even food didn't help.

At home we waited, antsy, for 11:00 to come—the end of her orientation activities for the night.

I know she's gonna call, I kept telling myself.

But the nightly news came and went. She didn't call.

Now, because I'd been an assistant dean of students at the University of Arizona, I knew enough not to call her. So I hung in there.

Seven days later she called. I was so excited that I yelled to Sande, "Honey, get on the phone. It's Holly!"

Then I realized I should act cooler than that, so I said with swagger, "So, hey, how are you doing down there at school? I thought about you just the other day."

Uh, yeah. Like I hadn't thought about her every single minute since we'd parted.

After we heard about freshman orientation week and how exciting college was, I had to ask her one question: "When we left and you turned and walked toward your dorm, what were you thinking?"

"That's easy, Dad. I was thinking you and Mom brought me up right, and now it's my time to do it right."

Boy, that's pretty good. That's the way to raise kids. Kids who can someday walk away, wave their hand, and do life on their own.

Start with the End in Mind

Parent, it's okay not to be perfect. It's okay not to have a perfect kid. What's most important is your presence along the road of life. Are you present with your kids? Are you paying attention to them? Are you noting and appreciating the positive things they do so they don't have to try hard to secure your attention through negative behavior? Kids crave attention through your time, encouragement, investment in their world, and having their back when they need it (which is far different from snowplowing their road).

> *Kids crave attention through your time, encouragement, investment in their world, and having their back when they need it (which is far different from snowplowing their road).*

Now that you understand who each of your kids is, why they formed the life mantras they did, and what you've had to do with it, you can clear the decks of negative behavior and turn that behavior around. All it takes is a little reality discipline— letting the real-life consequences do the talking instead of you.

If you take all you've learned from this book and apply the time-tested strategies in chapter 11 from this point forward, you'll do fine in your parenting. Someday your kids will gladly return home from wherever they roam, and all of you will tell stories about these current misbehaviors and laugh around the family dinner table. You'll hear stories of what your kids did behind the scenes that you had no clue about . . . and are grateful you didn't know.

I know, because I hear such stories around my growing family dinner table—with five kids, three sons-in-law, and four grandkids—all the time.

There's no better time than the present to start with the end you have in mind. Remember, you're rearing an adult who will have his or her own family someday.

The next time that kid of yours shoots off his mouth, imagine him sitting there at your dinner table, 20 years from now, with his own mouthy kid.

The daughter who does the perfect eye roll? Imagine her with her own teenager who's learned eye rolling from her best role model . . . her mother.

The kid who takes off on a joyride and dings the family car? He's now got hair streaked with gray from his own kid, who did the same thing with the family van.

Such a flash-forward would put today's troubles in perspective, wouldn't it?

Time indeed has wings. The older you get, the faster it seems to fly. What matters most, above "correcting" any misbehavior, is what happens to your relationship in the long term.

Someday it will be your turn to walk your kid to their college dorm. Will they be saying what Holly did: "You brought me up right, and now it's my time to do it right"?

As my wise coach friend said, "They don't care what you know until they know that you care."

Memorize those words and act on them, and you'll do just fine.

Bonus Section #1

Ask the Expert

What would Dr. Leman have done in those situations in chapter 1? Find out here.

Back in chapter 1, we looked at 12 situations of misbehaving kids to figure out what purpose their behavior served. Now let's take it a step further. If it had been *me* as the parent in that situation, what would I have done?

Behavior #1: Two-year-old electrical engineer

Buy some of those cheap plastic plugs for all the outlets your daughter can reach and insert them when she's napping. Then hide somewhere around the corner where she can't see you and let her try sticking her finger into each one until she's frustrated. Every kid gets tired of a game that doesn't work. And nobody wants to play to an audience that isn't there.

Behavior #2: Three-year-old toy manager

That child needs more time home with you, learning to share toys with a few neighborhood playmates, before he's ready for the larger group of preschool. Sure, you had that preschool picked out for years and he'll lose his treasured spot, but isn't your child's long-term best more important?

Also, when your child watches how you interact with others, are you kind? Do you willingly share things with others and treat them as important? Are you fair, or do you have to win? You are your toddler's best teacher.

> *Children are as unique as blades of grass, and that includes their readiness for any school.*

There's no rule that says you have to go to preschool to succeed in life. Many preschools have waiting lines of candidates because parents fear their kids won't have a competitive edge in life if they don't go. Don't try to keep up with the Joneses. Who are they anyway?

Children are as unique as blades of grass, and that includes their readiness for any school. So do what is right for your unique child right now, which is keeping him home and working more with him to smooth his rough edges. Then he'll have a better start at school with his peers because he's a little older and wiser. And so are you.

Behavior #3: Five-year-old defiant princess

Pick your battles wisely with this determined princess. Since the collared shirt was your idea and isn't a school uniform, weed those hated shirts out of her wardrobe and into a box under your bed for now. Don't give them to Goodwill yet, though, since kids often change their minds when they see what other kids wear. But collared shirts aren't something you climb up a battle hill and stake your victory flag on.

The night before the next school day, say, "When it's time for school tomorrow, I want you to wear whatever you'd like to wear. Just come out dressed at 7:30, and I'll have your favorite granola bar and juice box ready for you to take in the car."

Then you walk away. You leave it up to her whether she looks at her clothing choices the night before or scrambles to find something in the morning.

The next day you're ready to drive her to school in whatever she's wearing at 7:30, even if it's her pajamas. Because she still doesn't like the hubbub of kindergarten, she'll try to stall you.

But you're smarter. You smile outwardly at her weird outfit even though you're wincing inwardly at what others might think when they see it. "I see you're ready, as I asked. Here's your juice box and granola bar. I've got your backpack already in the car."

You hustle her off to the car and buckle her in her car seat before she even knows what happened. That day you are on time to kindergarten, and she's forced to mingle with the other kids.

What have you done as a smart parent? You've taken the collared shirt out of the mix (easy solution) and removed the dressing excuse (easy), so now your daughter will have to work harder to stall getting out the door.

When she balks tomorrow, you say and do the same things you did today. It won't take long before she sees you mean business.

Now comes the hard part—stage two. Instead of the loud "No," she'll try crying to tug at your mama heart.

"But I don't want to go," she'll say, complete with a fountain of manufactured tears.

Your answer: "Sometimes I don't want to go to places either, but I still do. If you want to talk about this further, I'm all ears tonight. But for now, we need to leave for kindergarten because it's our responsibility to get there on time."

Depending on how strong-willed your child is, you may have a few rounds of stage two defiance. But eventually your daughter will get used to the hubbub of kindergarten and fit right in with the rest of the pack.

Behavior #4: Six-year-old on the hot seat for bullying

Practice some deep breathing on the way to school and shake off your anger so you can greet the principal and parents with a firm handshake. Don't make any claims about your son's innocence or offer any excuses for the behavior he is currently accused of. At this point, you don't know what he did or didn't do, or what the other child did or didn't do. Simply ask for a recounting of the chain of events: what happened, who was involved, what adults were in the room, and so on. Also ask about anything that happened right before that event. If your son isn't the type to punch another child, as the other parents are claiming he did, there must be a reason for his behavior. Or, as can happen often, the other child had a lot to do with that reason or may even be lying to get your son in trouble.

It used to be that scuffles between kids were handled on the playground between the kids. Sure, there might be an occasional bloody nose or a few scratches, but then the kids came to terms with each other and came up with a solution.

Today parents are litigious. One scuffle between first-graders can become an all-out war in court between the parents. The term *bullying* is used loosely. True bullying is a pattern of a larger child or a group of children picking on an individual child, not a one-time occurrence.

The best thing you can do is gather the facts. If the principal is a good one—level-headed and concerned about justice, not about backing the most "popular" parent or one who gives the most philanthropy money to the school—he should already have done his homework. That should have included asking each boy individually what happened, then getting the boys together to restate what each says happened and to read their reactions *before* getting the parents involved.

> The best thing you can do is gather the facts.

Many scuffles at school, especially at such a young age, can be solved simply by the principal talking through the source of the conflict with the two children and having one or both apologize to the other. First-graders can be enemies one day and play during recess the next.

Whenever there are problems at school with students, it's in the best interest of the students, their parents, the teachers, and the principal to get the facts out on the table so you can work together toward a mutually beneficial and just solution. The fact that the parents are involved so quickly should raise a red flag about the seriousness of the situation, the principal's ability to deal with the situation, and the nature of the parents.

In this situation, after hearing the facts, ask for a quick time-out so you can talk with your son. Ask him what happened. If he did lose his temper and slug the other kid and admits to it, say, "You've gotten angry before. I get angry sometimes too. But why, this time, did you punch that kid? What happened right before that?"

Then, when you know the answer to that question, you regroup with the principal, the other kid, and his parents. It's best if both children then state—without interruption—their account of what happened. A moderator, such as the principal, should ask questions: "So when you were on the monkey bars, Nathan said X. What did you say?" By "retelling" the story and asking for a confirmation, lies can swiftly unravel and the truth will come forward. Better for it to happen now than down the road with both of you invested in attorneys.

On the way home, both you and your son will be keyed up. The best thing you can say is, "Well, I wouldn't want to go through that again, would you?" with a little laugh. Then add something like, "I think both of us need a break before we talk about this again. So how about a snack when we get home, and then we regroup after an hour or so and talk in the living room?"

When you step foot in your home, you both take that time. But an hour later, you follow through on what you said you'd do. "Okay, now that the dust has settled from that not-so-fun experience, I'd like to know . . . what do you think you could do differently next time if you had a situation like that happen again?"

Believe me, your six-year-old will pay attention. After all, he expected the parental hammer to come down, but you're asking his opinion instead.

"Uh, I know what I did was wrong, and I'm sorry, Mom."

Without a lecture from you, he's already accepting the responsibility for his actions, which he has stated are wrong. See how this works?

He continues. "I shouldn't have punched him. But I don't like it when kids tease me."

Your parental radar goes up. "So right before that, he teased you about something."

"Yeah." He slumps. "He said I didn't have parents."

"And he thought that because . . ."

He turns away. "Because you and Dad didn't come to our play."

And there it is—the reason for your child's misbehavior. Just when he was feeling alone in the world at school and probably a wee bit embarrassed because he was the only kid without parents there, a classmate honed in on his weakness.

"And you really wanted us to be there."

"Yup."

That, parent, is the naked truth of *why* the situation occurred. As hard as it is to hear, good for you for uncovering it now, in your child's early years, when the stakes are lower than they'd be if he were a 16-year-old who slugged it out with another kid.

You won't sleep well tonight as you wrestle with next steps. But knowing the truth—that your child craves your attention and involvement in his life, and that no one but you will do—is the foundation you can build on.

To build a cathedral, you have to start one brick at a time. The good news is, you can create that enduring structure together, and every minute you spend placing those bricks will be worth it.

Together you can look for ways to turn that negative energy that led to your son punching another kid into dialogue between the two of you that can fuel conversation and positive actions. Someday down the road you'll both look back at this moment and see it as a pivotal time in your relationship as parent and child.

Behavior #5: Eight-year-old space cadet

Leave that backpack out in the weather—rain, shine, or snow. Even better if there are a few of the neighbor's dog plops on it. She's the one who has to take the backpack to school in whatever shape it's in and explain to the teacher why her homework is unreadable. If you rescue her now, you're setting yourself up for years of even more rescuing. Now's the time to let the chips fall where they may . . . or let the backpack stay where it lies.

Just close the kitchen blinds so you can't see it out there and be tempted.

Behavior #6: Nine-year-old math homework actress

The instant that kid kicks up a fuss and begins her dog and pony show, say, "I'm sure you'll figure it out." Then exit stage left—out of sight and out of hearing so you're not tempted to go back to help her.

She'll likely try out any other parent in the home and then her siblings—oldest one first, since she knows he's more responsible. But you've already clued everyone in not to help her.

This may sound heartless, but it's the only way to figure out if your child really can't grasp math, is behind on math concepts, and needs assistance, or if she's merely lazy and doesn't like to do her homework.

Never allow your daughter's nightly escapades to be the thermostat that controls the temperature of your home.

Let a few days go by. Clue the teacher in that you're interested in how your daughter is progressing in math. If it seems like a problem, ask the teacher if she could refer you to some additional help for your daughter after school.

Never allow your daughter's nightly escapades to be the thermostat that controls the temperature of your home. It's not fair to you or to anyone else living there.

When you see her finally working hard on her homework, walk by and say, "It makes me so happy to see you working on your math. I know it isn't the easiest subject for you. But I believe in you. Good for you for tackling it right after dinner."

Now that's positive attention that will motivate her to work even harder, because secretly she loves it when she can make you happy.

Good job, Mom.

Behavior #7: 10-year-old cranky mess

I feel for the kid, who is getting bounced back and forth between two homes like a Ping-Pong ball. That's a rough existence. Even worse if it seems pointless. The kid's right. If his dad isn't paying any attention to him, why exactly is he there? Problem is, you can't always fight a court settlement. It's easier to insist on having shared custody—especially if any revenge against an ex is involved—than it is to carry it out.

Allow your son some breathing room. Realize he'll be cranky when he walks in the door and that his crankiness is a cry for attention: *Please notice me. Notice that I'm home. I need to know that I matter to you and you won't leave me.*

Give him a hug and a smile when he walks in the door, even if he seems to reject it. Have some of his favorite food ready (even if you're not a cook and have to microwave it) to welcome him home. Even if he doesn't eat it, it's the gesture that counts. Give him an hour and he'll reheat it.

> His crankiness is a cry for attention: Please notice me.

Sometime in the coming week, when he seems to be in a better mood, say, "I've noticed that you seem down on Sunday afternoons, when you get back from your dad's. I know it's been tough for you since the divorce. I'm often sad too. But I want you to know that I miss you when you're not here, and I'm glad when you come home. You're so important to me."

You didn't ask any questions like, "Why are you so down?" or "What's going on over there that makes you so cranky?" You're his parent, not a private investigator. You can't control what goes on at your ex's, only what goes on in your own home.

By simply stating what you did, you're paying positive attention and ensuring him of your love and care. You're also opening the door to talking about his feelings—without pointing out he's being such a crab—by saying that sometimes you feel sad too.

There's no such thing as an easy divorce. But together the two of you can work through the tough times and use them to bond you like superglue.

It doesn't mean that, at another time, you don't address his crankiness if it's aimed at you. There's a big difference between mouthing off at you *about* you and spewing in general in your hearing range because life doesn't feel fair. You should never, ever accept disrespect from your kids. But sometimes you have to extend to your kid what you would want yourself: some undeserved grace when you're in a tough spot.

Behavior #8: 11-year-old exit-stage-left magician

Your 11-year-old may be picking on his sister, but I'm certain Li'l Cutie is doing her part to irritate older brother. Just because she's younger and looks innocent doesn't mean that she *is* innocent. Babies of the family know exactly how to get their older siblings in trouble, and it usually includes yelling for Mom and Dad and looking helpless.

There's a reason *sibling rivalry* is such a familiar term to the average person . . . unless you're an only child, of course.

Here's what I suggest: The next time your baby calls, "Mom," don't come. That baby is far more resourceful than you can imagine and adept at getting her brother in trouble. If you don't show up, the drama dies for lack of an audience. Even more, I know that brother is somewhere within earshot so he can fully enjoy the drama that he thinks will unfold. When you don't show, the fun fizzles.

The quickest way to end a sibling fight is to lock 'em both in a room and say, "Don't come out until you resolve the issue."

If the baby comes fleeing to you, say, "Well, I'm sure you two can handle it," and walk away.

The stunned baby will likely follow you, with her secret shadow trailing to hear the fallout. But you enter another room, shut the door, and go about your business.

Without your attention, the fight will be short-lived. In fact, the quickest way to end a sibling fight is to lock 'em both in a room and say, "Don't come out until you resolve the issue."

Most of the time there's dead silence. The two eye each other, drop their heads, and get embarrassed. The fight that was only for your benefit is over quickly.

In short, give them attention when they're doing positive things. Stay out of their squabbles and let them work out a solution themselves. It's the fastest route to peace in the kingdom.

Behavior #9: 13-year-old sassy-mouth chameleon

Never let a child get away with showing you disrespect, and that includes mouthiness. You have the label *parent* for a reason. You are older and thus should be more mature and wiser. You need to pick the most opportune times for expressing your dissatisfaction with your child's behavior.

Here's what I mean. You accomplish nothing if you say, "How dare you talk to me like that. I pushed for 18 hours to give birth to you." Or, "Do you know who I am? I'm your *father*. You better show some respect."

Instead, let the 13-year-old hothead say her piece and then retreat with her usual dramatic flourish and thump of the door. You go take a walk, or better yet, go and resurrect that ancient punching bag from the dusty corner of the garage. I promise you'll feel better.

Stay out of the drama queen's space and collect your thoughts.

Stay out of the drama queen's space and collect your thoughts. You know it doesn't work to confront her. She fires back more of her sassy mouth, and your internal organs start to heat up. So you're going to do it smarter this time. For both her best long-term interest and yours, you're going to wait and be patient.

Later that night, she wants to go to her girlfriend's for their scheduled get-together. You, of course, are the taxi service.

"Mom, it's 7:00. Let's go," she says, and heads for the car.

After she sits in the passenger seat for a few minutes and you don't show, she whips back inside. "Mom! Let's go. I need to get to Ashley's."

"Not tonight," you say, and head for the TV room. You put up your feet, click the remote on, and start flipping through the channels.

She circles you, hopping from foot to foot. "Mom, what's wrong with you? I'm already late to Ashley's."

"We're not going."

"But why? I always go to Ashley's on Thursday nights."

Now is your teachable moment. "Because I don't appreciate the way you talked to me earlier, so I don't feel like going." You flip to another channel.

Recognition dawns. Her voice softens. "I'm sorry, Mom. You know I didn't mean that. I was just upset."

"I understand, and I forgive you. Thank you for apologizing."

"So, are we good now?" she says. "I can go to Ashley's?"

This is the hardest moment of all. You have to stick to your guns.

"Yes, we're good now, but you're not going anywhere tonight."

She'll beg, plead, cry—try any moves that have worked before—but you are immovable. She goes nowhere that night. She'll whine about the fact that her social life has ended. After all, she has the embarrassing duty of telling her friend that she can't come. Whether she blames you or invents another excuse, the result is the same. That girl is homebound for the night.

Even more, she knows you mean business. Sure, she might test you again . . . and soon. But if you continue to stick to your guns, she'll get the message. Talking back to you won't gain her anything. In fact, it'll misfire with repercussions that are definitely *not* in the best interests of her social life or anything else she wants to do.

Behavior #10: 14-year-old probationary angel

Let's talk turkey. Parents want happy kids and think it's their fault if their kid isn't happy. But are *you* always happy? Then why should your child always be happy?

Parents who try to provide their kids with a Disneyland experience aren't doing them any favors. Think about it. When your son gets his first job, will his supervisor's goal be to make him happy? Or will it be to get the work done and make customers or clients happy? Better that your child experiences a little unhappiness now rather than a lot of unhappiness later because he's grown up in a fantasy world that can't deliver in the real world.

I've always said, "An unhappy child is a healthy child." Unhappy children, if they aren't placated, come to understand that the world doesn't revolve around them. Others matter. They're not the center of the universe. Pretty important concepts for any child who will become a grown-up to learn, right?

So, let me ask you: What does your 14-year-old have that you didn't give him? He's got a roof over his head, at least three square meals and free access to all the snacks he could ever want, someone who does his laundry, a gaming computer at his beck and call, and his iPhone with a $100 iTunes gift card from Grandma, who felt bad he had to be locked away at home all by himself. Now he doesn't even have to go to school, though his straight-A sister does, and his parents are MIA all day so he can freely do what he wants.

That life may look good to him at first, but the positives of it will wear thin. We humans are social creatures. He's already feeling the lack of a social life since his new posse is in school and so are his childhood friends back at his old home. Texting can only go so far, since his buddies have to pay attention in school sometimes.

So even though you're busy with that new job, setting up your new abode, and all the other transitions that a move forces (including navigating a new grocery store and finding a hairstylist), he wants to make sure you pay attention to him when you get home. That's why he trashes the joint and doesn't do what you ask of him. Then you are forced to engage with him.

I want you to try something. It's called "the bread-and-water treatment."

I want you to try something. It's called "the bread-and-water treatment." At first you may think this is harsh, but bear with me and see how it plays out. After all, you are reading this book because your son's behavior is driving you a bit nuts, and you want to see it change, right? Then read on.

Invade his world with a short conversation. "I know switching schools and moving isn't easy for you, but you're not the only one who's having it hard. Your behavior is making our transition even harder.

"You are a part of this family—a family that works together and plays together. As such, you get certain benefits, like having a roof over your head, food to eat, and an allowance every month for clothing and fun with friends, like movies and after-school tacos.

"Your mom and I go to work at 7:00 every day and work until 5:30. Your sister leaves for school at 8:00 and comes home at 3:30. Your work is to do four to five hours of schoolwork a day so you can step back into classes in a month after you are off probation. Until you go back to school, you already know you won't leave this house unless it's on a family-approved outing with the rest of us.

"Since you have extra time at home that your mom and sister and I don't have, you also need to contribute to our family. I want you to do three things. On Tuesdays and Thursdays, make a simple dinner that's ready by 6:00. Do all of the laundry that's in the laundry room by Wednesday morning, including washing, drying, folding, and returning the stacks of laundry to the appropriate rooms. And vacuum the house twice a week—once during the week and once on the weekend."

You state your expectations simply. You don't follow them with any threats, such as, "If you don't, young man, I'll make your life miserable." Or, "You won't get to leave this house until you're 80." If you've backed down in the past, he knows you won't follow through on those threats.

Then you walk away and leave him in that mess of a bedroom.

What's that kid thinking? *Wow, I sure got off easy. I don't have to do anything. Dad will cool off by tomorrow and life will be back to normal . . . only I get to stay on vacation.*

He won't know what hit him until Tuesday, when he wanders into the kitchen and the whole family is MIA. All he finds is a note:

Brian, we didn't see the dinner you were supposed to make, so we went out for dinner at Outback Steakhouse. We'll be back around 8:00. See you then.

He stands there in shock, holding the paper. It takes a good half hour before he starts to root through the fridge for some leftovers. As he chomps on the cold spaghetti from the weekend, all he can think is, *I sure wish this was steak.*

> You state your expectations simply. You don't follow them with any threats.

Then Sunday rolls around. You hand out the weekly allowance to his sister, then hand your probationary angel a strangely light envelope.

He opens it and spots the quarter in it. "Hey, Dad, what gives?" he blurts out.

You shrug. "Oh, that's what's left after we used what we needed to go out to dinner Tuesday."

Your daughter, Brittany, flings herself at you and hugs you. "Thanks, Dad!"

Your son raises a suspicious eye. "What are you thanking him for?"

She smiles. "Well, you didn't do the vacuuming, so Dad paid me to do it."

Now you've hit your son where it really hurts. Not only did he lose all his allowance except for a quarter, but he lost it to his mortal enemy—his sister. And he knows she'll rub that fact in for the rest of his life.

I'll bet you a hundred bucks that boy will start to get busy around the house. And he isn't likely to pull another probationary-angel move either.

It's amazing how reality discipline works, isn't it? And look at you . . . no lecturing, no high blood pressure.

Behavior #11: 15-year-old joyrider

That boy got your attention, all right, but he needs a lesson in responsibility and accountability.

If he can't follow basic rules, such as, "One parent has to be in the car when you're driving with a beginner's permit" and "No friends are allowed in the car when you're driving with a beginner's permit," he has no business driving a vehicle that has the potential to kill himself or anyone else. Bluntly, he's not mature enough to be behind the wheel.

But back up to the moment when you got that phone call from the police. If it were me, I wouldn't have said, "I'll be right there, Officer." I would have had a friendly chat with that officer that went something like this: "Thank you for calling me, Officer. . . . No, my son did not have my permission to take the car when he went on that joyride with his friend. . . . I agree that this should never happen again. So I'd like you to do what you would to an underage driver who doesn't follow the rules. . . . Oh, you already told him that his beginner's permit would be revoked? Good. I don't think it's a good idea for him to be behind the wheel right now either. Maybe in a year or two he'll be more mature. . . .

"He wouldn't be able to get his license until he's 18? Even better. Do me a favor, if you will. Let my son sit there at the police station for a few hours. Then I'll show up. I want to make sure he understands and feels the weight of this situation."

If you had that kind of conversation with the officer—instead of the typical parent making excuses for the errant son—he or she would probably be shocked at how even-keeled you are. When you do come in to that station, the officer will be shaking your hand and addressing you with respect. Your son? He'll be sitting on a bench in the corner, looking like a hungry puppy left out in the rain.

He wanted your attention? Well, he got it . . . and then some. I doubt he'll be doing anything like that anytime soon.

Problem is, what he did isn't a small matter. He had four strikes against him: he took your keys without permission, was driving without an adult in the car, had a friend in the car, and hit another car. In baseball, the rule is "three strikes and you're out."

What do you do now? You're in a tight spot. You know how much he wanted to get his license . . . and that he's going to drive you crazy if he can't drive soon. But you're also embarrassed and more than a little scared. A dinged bumper is one thing. Raised insurance rates is another. And the potential that he could have killed the lady behind the wheel of the other car makes your heart race.

If you don't want this to happen again and you want your son to grow into a responsible adult, it's time for a teachable moment that he's going to feel for a while. You don't rescue him. You hold him accountable for his actions.

He can blame anybody in the world, including you for not going driving with him, and he will probably try. But the bottom line is that his own actions led to his downfall.

You don't rescue him. You hold him accountable for his actions.

So he doesn't get to try for his license until he turns 18. In between he'll wear out a lot of sneakers with long walks and have to ask for rides (embarrassing when you're 16 and 17 and all your friends are driving). Sure, you can take him some places, but your sole job isn't to be his chauffeur.

His senior year of high school, when he realizes he has to pay for going through a much longer driving school because of his earlier shenanigans, you don't rescue him. He has to get a part-time job to pay the fees that go beyond those you paid for his sister to get her license two years ago.

When he finally does get his license after he turns 18, he still doesn't drive because he has a hard time getting insured and then has to pay exorbitant rates.

Again, you don't rescue him. Yes, you can say something like, "We give your sister $100 a month toward her car insurance while she's in college, so when you do get insurance, we'll provide the same for you." But you don't snowplow his road and reward him for being stupid and impatient. If your son feels the weight of his choices (at his age, a couple of years of not driving will feel like an eternity), he will be a much wiser, more patient person long-term.

So stick to your guns, parent. You're doing the right thing.

When you feel like giving in, try taking a joyride yourself. It'll blow the dust out of your ears and return your parental common sense to its proper place. After all, this whole experience will be a lot tougher on you than it is on that son of yours.

Behavior #12: 17-year-old con artist

Wow, your 17-year-old con artist certainly has your number. She's using the fact that you care about her future—and what school she gets into—to manipulate you into doing work that she should be doing. Are those college applications yours or hers?

If she gets into one of those colleges you're applying for, will you go to school with her? Sit by her side in class and take notes? Write her papers? Take her tests? Do her laundry?

Did you also do her homework for her when she was growing up because it was too hard or too much?

Caught you, didn't I?

Here's a cardinal rule for parents: Never do anything for your children that they are capable of doing for themselves. If you do, you undercut the development of their self-worth.

You can't manufacture self-respect for your kids. They have to earn it for themselves. No one feels good long-term about things being done for them or handed to them that they should have worked for.

Does that mean you can't give your daughter some pointers? Listen to her ideas for what she wants to write for a college essay? Bring her some coffee for her late-night cram session before a test? Go with her to college visits?

No. You do all those things and more. You're her parent, after all. She'll need you ringside, cheering her on as she fights battles in life. But you never, ever do her the disfavor of snowplowing her road in life.

A student who can't be motivated to fill out her own college applications isn't ready for college yet. Maybe she needs a gap year to think about what she wants to do. Maybe she needs some work experience to face realities she can't escape as an adult—like rent, car insurance, gas for a vehicle, groceries, and taxes. Maybe she needs vocational training as a hairstylist instead of a four-year university.

> *You can't manufacture self-respect for your kids. They have to earn it for themselves.*

Allow those realities to do the talking, not you. They'll train her far better than any parental lectures ever will.

Bonus Section #2

Q & A with Dr. Kevin Leman: Thinking and Acting Your Way to Behavioral Change

---

The hottest questions parents ask . . . and expert, practical advice you can live by.

Irresponsible, Bratty Kids

Q: We had our son and daughter later in life and were really happy to finally have kids. But sometimes I wonder if we're doing too much for them. Lately we've been getting a lot of attitude.

The other day my son said to me, "What is your problem? Why isn't my history paper done? It's due tomorrow." And my daughter is often late for school and wants me to write notes for her so she doesn't get unexcused tardies. I really hate having to come up with something when I know it's because she was too lazy to get up on time or spent too long deciding what outfit to wear.

How can we stop this train and help our kids become more responsible and less bratty? Sometimes I feel like their servant.

A: Seriously, you do your son's homework for him? You make excuses for your daughter when she doesn't show up for school on time? Really? Are you going to follow them to college and their first job to make sure they're happy and comfortable every moment there too?

If you think you're doing those things for your kids, take a good look in the mirror. You're not doing them for your kids. You're doing them for you, because the thought of your son and daughter being unhappy, struggling, failing, and not being able to compete with their peers drives you crazy.

> *Doing anything for your kids that they could do for themselves actually accomplishes the opposite of what you truly want.*

But here's the irony. Doing anything for your kids that they could do for themselves actually accomplishes the opposite of what you truly want. It ruins their chance for success in life because it weakens their resolve, kills their resilience, tears down their self-concept, and diminishes their desire to do anything in life on their own.

If that's what you're after, keep doing what you're doing. If not, consider this: Talk to any successful person and you'll find struggle and failure aplenty in their past. Take me, for example. I was such a poor student that I was stuck in the low-reading group with the kids who ate paste and flunked a class twice in high school. The only way I could get into college was on probation. Most people thought I'd amount to nothing. But here I am, with a doctorate to boot—all because a wise mom let me experience some things in life the hard way to wake me up and get me on the right track.

If you snowplow the roads of life for your kids—doing things they could and should do for themselves, making all their decisions for them—you rob them of developing psychological muscles they need to not only contribute to society but be a decent human being.

Your kids need to struggle, fail, and feel the sting of their mistakes sometimes. Failure and mistakes are steps on the road to success. Look at it this way. If you're happy and everything is going well, are you motivated to change? No. It's when things aren't going well that you start thinking, *Hmm, that didn't work so well. Maybe I should try something different next time.*

The same is true for your child. An unhappy child is a healthy child. That unhappiness will prompt him to consider doing things differently . . . if you don't give in, feel guilty for his unhappiness, and fix the situation for him. If you do, you're not fixing the situation. You're making the next one, and the rest of his life, worse.

So stop doing your son's homework. Leave it right where he puts it on the table. When he says the next morning, "Why isn't it done?" you shrug.

"I don't know. Why isn't it done? You'd know that best, since it's your homework." Then go get busy doing something else.

He won't believe what he's hearing. He'll think you have his homework stashed somewhere and are fooling him. Then cold reality hits, and he panics. "But Mom, if I don't turn it in, I'll get an F. He's a tough teacher, and he won't cut me slack."

"Well, then you'll get an F."

"If I get an F, he'll tell my coach, and I'll be sidelined until my grades improve," he argues.

"I know you'll work it out somehow," you say.

He sweats all day until that history class, while you walk around at home with a big smile, knowing that kid might attack his homework as soon as he gets home.

When your daughter wants that note, say with a smile, "Sure, I'll write it." But here's what you write:

Dear Principal,
My daughter was too lazy to get out of bed this morning, so she's late to school. Please do to her what you do to kids who are late without a justifiable reason. Thank you very much.

Yes, she'll be embarrassed, especially if she's used to you writing notes for her and doesn't even look at it first. Just in case she does decide to look at that note, prepare in advance. Set your phone to silent and stash it far from you. Don't check her texts until the end of her school day.

Since you've gone to such lengths, it's highly likely that daughter of yours will be out of bed right when her alarm goes off tomorrow.

Don't snowplow your kid's roads. Every child needs to learn to shovel a little snow, even if they live in Southern California.

Chore Slacker

Q: We want our kids, who are 12 and 14, to have a good work ethic, so we assign them rotating chores. For example, in the month of January our 12-year-old is responsible for dishes on Wednesdays and Fridays, and our 14-year-old is responsible for vacuuming twice a week. In February they switch. We also give our kids a weekly allowance and expect them to buy their own school clothes because we want them to learn how to be financially responsible.

Lately, though, our 12-year-old is getting into a pattern of not doing his chores. When I confront him about it, he complains we give him too much work to do.

So we went the next step and fined him by taking money out of his allowance. For every night he misses, we deduct 10 bucks. It's not working. He's still missing his chores. Any suggestions? It's not that we couldn't do the work ourselves, but we want to raise responsible kids.

A: Good for you. You've got the right goal in mind. It's merely your follow-through that needs some work. If you're giving him a generous allowance, deducting 10 bucks probably isn't enough.

How much would it cost you to get a person to come in and vacuum your house for the night? Or spend an hour washing the dishes and cleaning your kitchen? Hop online and get an estimate of a professional service and print that out. Then, when it's time to provide his allowance, tuck that estimate inside and deduct the amount from his personal envelope.

He won't be happy. Then again, neither are you, because he's not doing his fair share at home. But this next week, that boy is likely going to be doing those dishes or vacuuming. If he doesn't, you go round two or three until there's nothing left in that envelope.

Stand firm on this one. You can't afford to back down.

If he really is so busy that he can't help his family out, he's too busy and needs to cut down on his extracurricular activities. The rule in our family was one activity per semester, since we had five kids. Otherwise, we never would have intersected except at the drive-through.

Don't Recognize My Kids after the Divorce

Q: I'm the parent of an 8-year-old and a 14-year-old. My husband split a year ago, and we're in the process of getting a divorce. I'm the one who had to tell my kids. Since then, my once well-behaved kids have become a mess. My daughter who used to be sweet and sunny is now a major drama queen who can't deal with anything.

And I don't even recognize half the words that fly out of my son's mouth . . . if he'll even talk to me.

I can't help but think, *This is my fault and my ex's fault, not theirs.* I even told them that. But they treat me like I'm the enemy, when all I'm trying to do is help them.

The other day my son hit the wall with his fist and yelled, "I hate you. I want to go live with Dad." All because I said I couldn't order the pizza he wanted to eat with his friends. It didn't matter that we had a whole fridge of good food. He couldn't have what he wanted.

That really hurt. Believe me, I wanted to send him to his dad . . . permanently. But I love both my kids, and I know the atmosphere at my home is much better. I won't even go into the parade of affairs my ex had on the side, or the latest woman he lives with right now. My kids don't know about those, and it's all I can do to keep my mouth shut.

When it seems like I'm doing everything wrong, what can I do right? I need some help here.

A: There's no such thing as an easy divorce—for anyone involved. Kids of divorce feel like a dried-out turkey wishbone after Thanksgiving, with Mom pulling at one end and Dad at the other. They may think:

- "Why did *my* family have to fall apart?"
- "If Mom and Dad don't love each other, will they no longer love me?"
- "If Dad leaves, will I not see him again?"
- "Is this my fault? Do they hate me?"
- "What if we can't keep our house? Will I have to move? Change schools?"
- "Will Mom and Dad split us kids up? I don't always like my sister, but I want to live with her."

Most parents launch into the "it's not your fault" frenzy, thinking that'll be easier on the kids. "This is between us, the adults," they say. "It has nothing to do with you."

Nothing to do with me? It has everything to do with me, a kid thinks. Such a sucker punch tears life apart as she knows it. To protect herself, she adopts one or more common defense mechanisms:

- *She hides out or acts like the divorce doesn't matter.* She thinks, *If I lay low, maybe this will all blow over.* She conceals her feelings and deals alone with terrifying questions such as "What if Mom leaves too?" At night she quietly cries herself to sleep.
- *He becomes the adult.* When Mom becomes fragile, he tries to calm the ruffled waters and works hard to spend equal time with each parent so neither will feel left out.
- *He gets angry or she becomes a drama queen.* He strikes out at everyone around him to purposefully get attention. She overreacts because of her emotionally messy state and boatload of hurt.

When you're hurting too, what do your kids need most from you?

They need you to be the adult.

Divorce has dropped a bomb on your family, so your son will understandably be upset—more so if he's already part of the hormone group. So give him some grace, but don't excuse disrespect and foul language. Though the heat of the moment isn't the best time to take on negative behaviors, the next day is fair game.

Say to him, "Let's circle back to what happened yesterday. I know you're hurting, but what you said really hurt me. I'm your mother, not your psychological punching bag. We *will* get through this tough time together, but I want to do that in a healthy way. I'll do my part the best I can, and I need you to do your part the best you can too. Can we agree on that?"

Be the decisive leader your kid needs—supportive, understanding, positive, action oriented—and you'll provide a stable environment even in a stressful time.

They don't need to be bounced around like a rubber ball.

Guilt is the propellant for most lousy decisions after a divorce, so make as few changes as possible. Yes, you might need to switch housing or school districts, but keep things as close to "normal" as you can for your child—including staying connected to old friends.

With most divorces, parents want to do the 50/50 kid split, but that approach takes a toll on already stressed kids. That's why—as improbable and crazy as it sounds—I tell divorcing couples, "If you're so high on having to spend equal time with your kids, then you two move from place to place and let the kids stay in their own home." After all, who's the adult here?

They don't need to play the "Dad versus Mom" game.

Your ex isn't likely your favorite person, but don't use your kids as a sounding board for your squabbles. Putting down your ex is only asking your kids to make him into "Father of the Year." So for their sake, extend an olive branch—as much as he might not deserve it. Don't extract information about what they did at your ex's or who was there. You aren't licensed to be a private eye.

Instead, provide a warm environment (food helps!) and some non-stressed space to return to. If they want to talk, believe me, they will—of their own volition—and you'll learn a lot more than you would through any extraction technique known to humankind.

Power Struggle with Toddler

Q: We're having a major power struggle with our three-year-old. She's been potty trained since she was eighteen months old and has slept through the night. But lately she's been getting up five or six times a night to go potty. Every time she does, she wanders down the hallway to find us and interrupts anything we're doing.

My wife and I are exhausted and frustrated. We have no alone time anymore, and we've both got dark circles under our eyes. I don't think there is a physical problem because after the third or fourth time every night, she'll say, "Mom, Dad, are you mad?"

I think she's manipulating us. How can we make her stay in bed?

A: You're right. She *is* manipulating you, and you're falling for it.

You have a strong-willed child, no doubt about it. But she didn't get that way all by herself. Someone in the family taught her that misbehavior. I won't point any fingers, but perhaps it's one or both of her parents.

Now, there's a one-in-a-million chance that there's a medical reason your daughter has to go wee-wee that much. It might be good to ask the pediatrician at her next checkup. However, if that was the case, that child could get up, go potty without all the extra fanfare, and go back to bed.

You have a strong-willed child, no doubt about it. But she didn't get that way all by herself.

In your case, I highly doubt there's a medical reason. It's all about pulling your parental chain. A big clue is in her question: "Mom, Dad, are you mad?" That cherub of yours knows exactly what she's doing. If you've said "No, stay in bed" to her drink requests and said no to her requests for a fifth teddy bear to be added to her nighttime animals after she's already in bed, but you've said yes to going potty, that little *aha* cemented itself in her brain. *So if I say I have to go wee-wee, then I can get up and explore the house and find out what those big people are doing.* And she has you over the proverbial barrel since you know kids have to go wee-wee, so it's impossible for you to say no.

Parent, beware. Any pattern you set now will stay and might continue until she leaves for college. So there are times when you have to draw the line as a parent.

My firstborn, Holly, was strong-willed. One day when she was misbehaving, I put her in a chair in her bedroom and told her to stay in that seat. She didn't. She came out and followed me. The second time I put her back in that chair, I went out and closed the door. When she tried to get out, I held the door shut.

I can hear some of you saying, "How could you? You might've done damage to your daughter's psyche."

No, that determined child is a very successful superintendent of a large school district today.

I'd never give you any advice that I wouldn't use with my own child. So here it is: you need to play hardball now, while you're still holding all the cards. Fact is, right now you can physically make her stay in that room. If she doesn't learn now, what will she be like as a teenager?

As soon as a child knows you can make them stay in a room, they will back off. Most tykes don't like the idea of a door being closed. That's why when they go to bed, they say, "Leave the door open, Daddy." And many kids like a night-light, which of course keeps the monsters under the bed from climbing out.

Since children crave routine and find safety in it, set a bedtime routine now. Then don't let that powerful child work you.

Sande and I had Holly when we were young and dumb parents. She indeed was our experimental guinea pig, and we learned a lot about what not to do with the next four kids we'd have.

When Holly was getting ready for bed, she'd do her best to drag out the bedtime routine. She'd point to various things in the room and say, "I want that." So I'd lovingly go and get that stuffed animal. As soon as I was back, she'd point to something else. "I want that." So off Dad would go to get it.

By the time I was taking her to bed, I barely had room for little Holly in my arms. I was staggering under the load of so many stuffed animals and other paraphernalia. That kid who was shorter than a yardstick had ol' Dad wound around her finger until I took my own advice as a psychologist.

After you say "Good night. I love you," that's it. The end. Finale. The kid stays in bed, and you go on with the rest of your adult life.

So establish a bedtime routine. It might be reading a book or singing a song or saying a prayer together, if you're a person of faith. Perhaps you then give your daughter a good-night kiss and hug and plug in the night-light. But after you say "Good night. I love you," that's it. The end. Finale. The kid stays in bed, and you go on with the rest of your adult life.

Don't set yourself up for continuing failure. Be brief, loving, and firm in your rituals. Then say good night.

If she gets out of bed to go potty and trails down the hall after you instead of returning to her room, tell her, "Go back to your room. It's bedtime." If she doesn't, you usher her back inside her room and close the door. You don't tuck her back in. The bedtime routine is over. If she tries to come out that door, you hold it shut until she gets tired and falls asleep on the floor.

Since she's used to manipulating you and having it work, it might take a few times of doing this to establish a new nightly routine. But remember, slow and steady wins the race. Be like the tortoise, not the hare.

Allergic to Homework

Q: My 10-year-old boy is all action and hates to sit down and do homework. He brought home a report card with one A (in gym), two Bs, two Ds, and one F. When he did, I almost cheered—at least half of the grades were acceptable. Does that tell you anything about how bad his grades are in general?

How can I encourage him to do his homework? He seems to do better on tests, but he never gets the homework done or turned in.

A: That boy of yours ain't dumb, Mama. He's distracted. When he sits down to crack open that homework, he thinks of something else he'd rather do—like play baseball with the neighbor boys in his backyard.

Here's what I'd try. Have a chat with that boy of yours. "Ethan, I know that doing homework isn't your thing, but it's a necessary part of school, like me getting groceries is necessary in order for you to have dinner and snacks. So we're going to try something different. I'd like your opinion on this. If you could pick one spot at home to do your homework where you won't be distracted by other things, where would that be?"

When you ask your child's opinion, you get his attention. That's far better than issuing the parental ultimatum: "Your grades are terrible. Tomorrow when you get home from school, you'll have half an hour to play before starting your homework. And you're not going to bed until you get it done."

Those kinds of threats won't do either of you any good. Your son knows you might be on the bandwagon for a day or two, but then you'll get distracted with other things. Staying up late and not getting sleep won't help either of you—in concentration or in mood.

Instead, to help your son make homework a priority, you need the right setup:

- *A place.* Your son needs a place of solitude that is *his* spot. Maybe it's a table in your guest bedroom or a cozy spot in your basement where you add a remnant rug since he loves to lie on the floor. Make sure that spot is well-lit so he doesn't feel sleepy and that it's free of distractions—like a blaring TV or his whiny sister.

- *A set time slot.* You know your son's best schedule. Does he need a short break after school to release all that physical energy he has stored up? Most students can't go straight from school to another study session. They need a couple hours of break time, with some food in between. I suggest that you help him set a two-hour time frame, say 6:00 to 8:00, where he concentrates on doing his work (minus any electronic devices he doesn't need to do the work).

- *Prioritizing.* Some children aren't naturally organized and need to be pointed in the right direction. For the first week, take five minutes at the beginning of his study time to look at his assignments (most schools have them online) and help him prioritize what to finish first. Tell him, "You know what needs to get done. I know you can do it. I believe in you." Then, as hard as it is, exit his space and let him accomplish what he needs to in that time frame. After the first week, he should know the ropes about how to check on his assignments, so you shouldn't be involved.

- *Noninterference.* You don't check on him or peek around the corner to see what he's doing. You don't allow his little sister to invade the basement or any other space that is solely his during that time frame.

- *A timer.* When 8:00 hits, a buzzer or a light goes off (think Pavlov's dog programming here). Homework time is over. Whatever he got done is whatever he got done.

These simple steps will teach your son that there is a time and place to do homework, and he needs to accomplish it within that window. From 8:00 on is his time to engage with the rest of the family or do activities he wants to before his 10:00 bedtime.

"But Dr. Leman, you don't know my kid," you're saying. "He'll use that time to do anything but study, especially if I'm not watching him."

Well, then you move to the next stage. "Ethan, I see by your report card that your grades and homework still aren't improving. We've already set a quiet place and a time window for you to do your homework, but your teacher says it's still not getting done. What else do you think we could do that would help you get it done?"

Give your son time to come up with options. Many of them will likely be crazy, including, "Quit school because I hate homework."

You know how much he loves playing baseball with the neighbor kids after school, but you've got a teachable moment here. You gently lower the boom.

"You seem to have difficulty concentrating during those two hours we set aside. So for the next week, instead of playing baseball, I'd like you to have a snack and then some quiet time by yourself before dinner. Let's see if that helps you settle in to study during those later two hours. You can play baseball on Saturday instead, if the boys have time."

Okay, now you have your active son's attention. "No, I'll pay attention. I'll get my work done. Really, I will."

But you stick to your words. For the next five days, your son doesn't play baseball. He has some quiet time to himself. You stick to the two-hour homework slot.

By the end of those five days, that boy will be zipping through his homework in the two-hour slot because he wants his baseball time back. Once his head is in the game and he's used to the homework routine, you'll be amazed at how those grades will improve.

Ungrateful Complainers

Q: I have a 15-year-old daughter and a 13-year-old son. Both complain all the time that I don't give them enough. They want more. More clothes, more pizza nights out, more video games. I don't have enough snacks, or the right kinds of snacks, in the house.

I'm so sick of their complaining. I give them a small allowance every Sunday to cover a few treats with friends and an occasional lunch at school if they forget to pack one from home, but they're back with their hands out by Tuesday.

I work hard, and I'm not made of money. How can I halt this "gimme, gimme" behavior and make my kids grateful for what they have?

A: You can't make your kids grateful. They have to be grateful on their own. However, you can help them realize that money doesn't grow on trees through some practical techniques.

First, make a list of everything you normally buy for your kids on a monthly basis and approximately what each item costs. Add up the figures and you'll likely be surprised. You say you're not made of money, yet you still buy all those things for your kids. So why not help them learn to be responsible by giving them what you spend on them each month and letting them make their own purchases?

Lest you think that's a crazy idea, I did it with all five of our kids. We gave them a good allowance every month, but they bought all of their personal stuff—clothes, deodorant, toothpaste, makeup, shoes, and so on. As a result, they became very good shoppers. Even when they were in college, they sought out discount stores and bought larger quantities of things they knew they'd need at a far cheaper price, then stored them in the closet or under their bed.

When your kids control their own money, they'll begin to distinguish between basic needs and wants. They'll also learn to make wise, age-appropriate choices and to be responsible for them long-term.

"But Dr. Leman," you're saying, "you don't know my kids. They'd spend all that money the first week and then have nothing for the rest of the month."

Then they don't have money for the rest of the month. They might be squeezing that toothpaste tube hard, and they might not be able to buy shoes to go with that new outfit.

Sure, they might not make good choices in the beginning, but there's no better place to learn how to save money and spend money wisely than at home. When kids are spending their own money (well, yours, but gifted to them each month), they'll naturally begin watching how much items cost and will get an eye-opening education.

> *There's no better place to learn how to save money and spend money wisely than at home.*

Second, teach them how to save money. I told my kids, "If you save a dollar this week, I'll match that dollar." That way they could get used to the idea of putting aside money for a rainy day and taking advantage of an employer matching fund someday.

Understanding the value of a buck will also nudge your kids in the direction of becoming more grateful for what they have in an increasingly self-entitled world.

Third, role-model generosity. If you see a need in someone's life, do your best to meet that need. Help the elderly next-door neighbor grocery shop or buy a treat for her. Stock shelves at your local food pantry once a month. Being in contact with people who have far less can be a wake-up call for entitled kids. When they see how others live, they'll start to see that even the needs they consider *basic* would be a dream come true for many others on the planet.

Sassy-Mouthed Kids

Q: Lately I've had this uncontrollable urge to buy some duct tape . . . for my kids' mouths. I'm tired of being the human garbage can for their attitudes and sass. Any time I ask them to do something, they say, "Why?" Like I'm asking them to do something huge, when it's only cleaning up the toothpaste remnants on their bathroom sink.

How can I curb their mouthiness? I've had it.

My girlfriend says I ought to be grateful. Her kids are far worse than mine. But seriously, do I have to live like this until they're 18? My kids are only 9 and 11.

A: You weren't put on this earth to be a garbage can or a rug to be stepped on. And you don't have to even consider living like this for another 24 hours, much less until they are 18. Such behavior has to stop.

I noticed that you said "their" bathroom sink. If they have a bathroom separate from yours, who cleans it normally? You? If so, you need to stop. Let it get super grubby, and let their toothpaste run out. Put your toothpaste where they can't find it.

When those mouthy kids come to you and say, "Mom! Where's the toothpaste? We don't have any toothpaste," you say casually, "Oh, really? Well, use the toothpaste on the sink. There's plenty."

Then you walk to another room and shut the door. You don't go shopping for toothpaste that day or even the next day. Don't worry, their teeth won't rot in that amount of time. Just give your dentist the heads-up to give an extra-special cleaning on their next appointment.

When they say again, "Where's the toothpaste? How come you didn't buy any?" you say, "As I said, there's plenty on the sink. I didn't need to buy more."

"Oh, that's so gross," they reply.

"Maybe. Then again, it's your bathroom." Again, you turn your back and walk away.

I bet you anything those two will confab in the bathroom and try to talk each other into cleaning that messy sink. Somehow it'll get done.

Even better, have those two buy the next tube of toothpaste out of their allowances. They won't be as likely to waste it. In fact, they'll probably be fighting over who didn't roll up the toothpaste tube and who is using too much. "We're going to have to pay for it, you know."

You should never take sass from your kids. When they talk to you disrespectfully, there must always be a real-life consequence that fits the situation. They don't go to that next outing. You don't take them to get fruit smoothies. And they have to clean their own bathroom, sink included, which they should be doing anyway at their ages. After all, are *you* making the mess in there, or them? Hold them accountable for their own mess.

Then again, you might want to keep some duct tape around. It would come in handy for certain moments, wouldn't it?

Kindergartener Attached to Mom's Leg

Q: Every time I get close to the kindergarten door, my son wraps himself around my leg and refuses to let go. If it only happened once, it wouldn't be so embarrassing. The first time I had to walk back to my car with him still attached and take him home. But it still happens every morning, and it's been a month now. I have to inch my way forward with his body literally hanging from my leg, then pry his fingers off once I'm through the classroom door. If I don't sprint out of there when I'm free, he'll attach himself again.

What should I do? The kid's got to go to school.

A: You're right. Kids do have to go to school, but maybe your son's not ready. Just because he's five doesn't mean he's ready for kindergarten. Maybe he needs another year at home with you first to gain a bit of maturity and to see other kids his age going to school before he sees it as a good place to be.

Also, that kid has your number. You've likely had his back a little too much, smoothing his path in life. He doesn't want to let go of the one sure bet he has to journey into an atmosphere of unknowns. He wouldn't cling to your leg like a spider monkey unless it worked. Clearly, it worked the first time, since he got to return home with you.

That first day of kindergarten, his "aha" kicked in: *If I cling to Mom's leg long enough and refuse to let go, she'll have to take me home with her. Then I can do whatever I want at home.*

So why not have a chat with your son to start your investigation?

"Honey, what do you think about kindergarten?"

If all he talks about is not liking sitting in his seat, or having to follow directions when all he wants to do is play, he's likely not ready. Most kindergartens have an "Is Your Child Ready for Kindergarten?" checklist. If you don't already have one, ask for a copy. Read it to see if your son indeed fits that list. If he is missing some key factors for readiness, he'd benefit greatly from another year at home with you first.

Don't think of it as holding him back. Instead, if you delay sending him for a year, you are giving him the best possible chance of success academically and socially with his peers. He'll be better prepared to pay attention in class, and he won't be one of the younger boys. With boys especially, who tend to mature later than girls, being older will allow him to hold his own better in the physically competitive world of males.

On the first week of kindergarten, it's not uncommon for kids—especially firstborns and onlies who want to know details and the road map—to cling to their mommies and daddies. It's a new experience, so why wouldn't they be a bit anxious?

Think of them as baby birds that poke their heads up out of that warm, feather-lined nest and peer out at the big outside world. They're not sure yet what to think, and many of them don't want to move from their cozy spot. In that nest Mama does everything for them, including bringing those delicious, fat worms for breakfast. So Mama or Papa Bird has to give them a nudge out of the nest to try their wings.

On the first week of kindergarten, it's not uncommon for kids to cling to their mommies and daddies.

If your child has gone to preschool, he's less likely to be anxious about entering the kindergarten door, unless he's had a negative experience in preschool. If he hasn't gone, that kindergarten door is the first big nudge out of the nest.

Also, it's helpful to talk to the teacher about your concerns and get her feedback about what she sees in the class. Is your son ready for such work? Kindergarten isn't merely the play environment it used to be. Real work and preparation for future studies happen there.

If you both agree your son should be there, set up a strategy with the teacher. For example, instead of you walking your son in, perhaps you pull up to the kindergarten door in your car. Your teacher or an assistant opens the passenger door, helps your son out of his seat belt, picks up his backpack, and walks him into kindergarten without fanfare.

Remember what I said about your son wanting your attention? His behavior is purposive. But if you're removed from the situation and his "kindergarten grid" thinking, getting him through that door and engaged with the other kids might be a whole lot easier. So why not give it a try?

Wait and see. Soon that son of yours won't even have time to say goodbye to you as he leaps out the car door and goes running into kindergarten. After all, his friends are waiting for him, and so is the temporary class mascot—the real frog in the zipped cage that he gets to greet every morning for a month if he shows up on time.

What could be more exciting?

Unmotivated Kid

Q: I'm embarrassed to ask this, but I'm desperate. My misbehaving son is 21, and he's still living with us. Any time I ask him to help out around the house, he says, "Why should I?" When I prompt him to get a job instead of hanging out with his friends, he says, "I *do* look for jobs. I just don't find any. Stop pressuring me."

He went to community college after high school but quit after only a semester. He's been doing basically nothing since. How can I motivate him to get moving in life, and to show some appreciation for what we do?

A: You can't motivate him to do anything. Motivation has to come from within. But you certainly can do a few things to move him in that direction.

I understand that you're doing what parents have historically done for generations—given their kids a roof over their heads and food to eat. Let's be blunt, though. Your son has clearly overstayed his welcome and is taking advantage of your kindness in your not-so-palatial mansion. He's not in school, and he's not working outside the home. He's only hanging out with friends, living the good life.

Let me ask you: Where is he getting the money to live that good life? Likely it's from you. But your son isn't 10 anymore, and he's moved past you needing to give him an allowance. He's an adult.

When you open the door for anyone—relative or not—to live with you, you should at least have a verbal contract that this is a short-term solution. With that basic understanding in place, there is a clear-cut end of the relationship after the agreed-upon period is over.

Motivation has to come from within. But you certainly can do a few things to move him in that direction.

You probably didn't have that kind of defining conversation. He simply quit school and settled into easy street in your home.

Now is the time for a straightforward conversation. "I know life isn't turning out the way you thought it would. But you've been out of high school for three years and out of full-time community college for over two years. It's time for you to get a job and your own place. You need your space, and we need ours. So give me a time in the next 30 days when you can move into your own apartment. We'll stay in contact with you, because you're our son and we love you. But you need to move on in life."

That's the wake-up call your couch potato needs right now. Even more, he needs you not to back down. When those 30 days are up, if plans aren't moving along, you move his possessions out to the lawn and change the locks on the door.

You don't respond to angry phone calls. You don't help him find a place or a job. He needs to do those things on his own. He may have to make his way through his groupies to find one he can temporarily stay with. Such friendships will wear thin fast if he follows his patterns of taking and never giving. Soon he'll be forced to grow up and become an adult, which includes finding a job, making money, and paying rent.

I know this sounds harsh, but his mouthiness says he lacks respect for you. Since he's 21, you aren't going to train that out of him unless you say what you'll do and then do what you've said.

So let reality do the talking for you after your initial pronouncement of the terms of his stay.

Continuing to let him live with you is one of the worst decisions you could make as a parent. You'll become an enabler, and you'll lessen the chance of him becoming the man he should be . . . not to mention the responsible husband your someday daughter-in-law deserves and the engaged, accountable father your someday grandchild needs.

Door Slammer

Q: My 14-year-old is a notorious slammer. Anything she doesn't like, off she goes to her room and slams the door. I hate it, but I'm kind of used to it. However, now we live in a fairly small condo, and our neighbor has mentioned the noise twice to me. Thankfully, she's been nice about it, but I can tell it's really starting to bother her.

Other than taking the door off the hinges, which feels like an invasion of my daughter's privacy and space, what can I do? I've asked her over and over again *not* to slam the door. But she still does.

Any advice?

A: Sure, I've got lots of advice.

There are these wonderful thick felt circles with adhesive on one side that can do wonders in the doorjamb as sound mufflers. I have a friend who lives in an apartment in Los Angeles who uses them and has even gifted them to a particularly noisy next-door neighbor, putting a cute poem on her door to ease any potential friction. They're easy to order, cheap, and easy to install. Tear the backing off the circle and stick it on.

If your daughter is only slamming her door because the sound is cathartic when she's upset, or she's doing it to get your attention and make you pay for how terrible the world is to her at that moment, those circles might do the trick. Don't say anything. Don't give her attention for such negative behavior. Simply install those sound deadeners when she's not home.

If door slamming continues to be an issue, solicit the help of that kind neighbor. The next time she comments on the noise, say to her, "You know what? That drives me crazy too. I've asked her not to do that and even installed some felt circles to deaden the sound. But I'm her mother, and she's having trouble listening to me. The next time you see her, would *you* comment on how the door slamming bothers you? I would greatly appreciate it."

You can bet that neighbor is going to be eagle-eyeing your daughter's whereabouts. As soon as your 14-year-old steps outside, she's toast. That neighbor has her in her sights. It won't be easy for your daughter to wriggle out of that one. She'll be gently closing her door for a long time, because she won't want that neighbor to track her down again.

Problem solved.

You can smile. You didn't even have to bribe your other next-door neighbor with brownies to get out his tools and take your daughter's door off. You simply let real-life consequences reign and take care of the misbehavior.

It's a win-win all around. Your daughter keeps her privacy, which is important to teenagers. You keep your sanity and your hearing. Your neighbors are happy. And Amazon sales go up from your felt circle purchases.

By the way, those felt circles also work great on closet doors and kitchen cabinets, if you have other slammers in the family.

Shopping Tantrums

Q: My son turned four in February. Any time I take him to the store, he pitches a fit. It starts because he sees something he wants and I won't buy it for him. I'm not a money tree. But he's too big to sit in the front of the cart now. He's using his own two feet, so he's harder to control.

I end up leaving my cart of groceries or whatever in the middle of the store and hustling him out. He's made such a fuss in so many stores that I'm embarrassed to go to them anymore. I'm starting to run out of new grocery stores, even though I live in an urban area.

Any tips to curb that obnoxious misbehavior?

A: *Tip #1:* Leave him at home whenever possible. There's no need for every shopping expedition of yours to be tantrum laden. You deserve a break too. Solicit the help of your partner or a friend to stay with him.

If your son sees you getting ready to go out, he'll likely say, "Mommy, are we going?"

You lean down and say, "Mommy's going. You're not."

Then comes the famous line: "But why, Mommy?"

Here's the teachable moment. "Because you make a fuss every time we go to a store. So I'm not taking you today. You are staying home."

Note that you don't say, "I'm *never* taking you to a store again," since that would be impractical and unrealistic. But to a four-year-old, having to stay home from that one outing will feel like Buzz Lightyear's "To infinity and beyond!"

He'll fuss. He'll pitch a fit right in your own living room. You'll shoot an apologetic look to your spouse, Grandma or Grandpa, or your friend, but out the door you'll go. You'll have a grand old time in that store with your head held high.

But here's the kicker. You don't let any guilt you feel for leaving your screaming son behind propel you into purchasing a treat for him. Do you want to reward misbehavior or nip it in the bud?

You arrive home, and your son is back to normal and excited to see you. He's long forgotten his tantrum from an hour ago.

"So what did you get me, Mommy?" he asks.

"Nothing," you answer simply.

His face darkens. His fists clench. "Why? You *always* get me a treat."

Another teachable moment is here. "Because I didn't appreciate the fit you threw when I was going out the door."

He'll plead, he'll cry, but you stand firm. No treat that day, including the ice cream you had reserved as a surprise for him.

To train a child up right, you don't accept or reward negative behavior. Yes, he may be young, but he's not dumb. He's watching everything you do and learning how to work you.

> To train a child up right, you don't accept or reward negative behavior.

If you've ever given in to one of his tantrums and purchased the item he grabbed merely to shut him up so people wouldn't stare at you, he recorded that moment as a victory. If he's continued his tantrums, it's because that action is beneficial to him. He got a reward from it—a new toy or a food treat.

When you don't play his game and his misbehavior is no longer beneficial, he'll quit. You simply have to stick to your guns and not get worn down. Give in once and you'll start over at square zero.

Tip #2: When you do have to take him to the store, have your game plan already in place. If he throws a tantrum right in the aisle of Walmart, complete with kicking and screaming and flailing, leave him on the floor and walk away. Go around the corner and "disappear"—so your child can no longer see you, but you can still keep an eye on him. If another customer is entering the aisle, feel free to shake your head and say, "Some people's children . . ."

Something magical will happen. That boy of yours will realize his Mommy audience is missing and he is all alone. He'll scramble up off that floor and go running pell-mell in the direction he saw you disappear. He'll be yelling all the while, "Mommy! Mommy! Don't leave without me!"

When you do regroup with your vociferous youngster, do something he doesn't expect. Don't walk toward him. Instead, walk out the door and to the parking lot.

He'll follow, looking confused. "Mommy, don't we have to get something?"

"Not today," you say, and open the car door.

In he goes, bewildered and deflated. "But I *always* get a treat at the store."

"Not today. Today we're going home."

Note the *always* in your son's talk. Children thrive on routine, and when it's interrupted they are thrown off course, especially if they are firstborns or onlies.

You drive straight home, get him out of the car, and then go about your business.

Your four-year-old won't know what to do. His world is off-kilter, no longer revolving on its well-established axis.

"If I am gooder, can we go back to the store?" he pleads.

"Not today," you repeat.

He slumps. That boy of yours has learned something new about his mama today—that she has a steel backbone.

Good for you, Mom. Keep doing things like that and you'll get that boy retrained.

School Quitter

Q: My 15-year-old announced yesterday that he's done with school. Then he went back to bed and missed the bus. Today he didn't get up either. He's a big boy, five foot ten, and stronger than me. I can't physically force him to go to school tomorrow. So what can I do or say to get him out of bed and moving? Ideas?

A: Certainly. A cattle prod might do the trick.

Seriously, a lot of 15-year-olds don't feel like going to school either, but they still get up and go. *Something* is fueling your son's sudden declaration. Asking him questions, though, won't get you anywhere. It will only firm up his anti-school stance and burrow him farther under those bedcovers. But a few things will give you clues.

Clue #1: If your socially networked son isn't texting much, it's likely something bad happened at school. He's trying to stay off the grid until it blows over.

This is when it's helpful if you know the parents of his friends. You don't embarrass him by calling them and asking outright if they know about anything that happened at school. Instead, you place a friendly call to say, "Oh, hi, Sandy. How are you?" That's all it will take for Sandy to say, "Well, I'm fine. But how about you? I heard Sam got in some trouble at school. . . ."

Then you know there's a definite reason your kid doesn't want to return, and you hear all the details secondhand. He's probably embarrassed and doesn't want to face the pack or you after what happened.

Clue #2: He sleeps all the time and doesn't come out of his room. Yes, he's a growing teenager and can sleep a lot, but this is beyond his norm. He doesn't want to interact with anyone.

It's normal for teens to be tired and overemotional in surges due to hormone changes, but if this is a complete change of behavior and it continues, pay attention. It's possible that he's experienced failure, rejection, or betrayal, and it's catapulted him into discouragement.

If you're seeing such major changes in his behavior, have a conversation with him, even if it's one-sided at the moment. "I notice you're sleeping a lot lately, and you seem a little down. If there's ever anything you want to talk about, find me. I'd like to help."

You don't push for information or linger. You say your piece and give him a couple minutes to respond. If he doesn't talk, you say simply, "I love you. Nothing will ever change that." And then you leave him to his man cave.

If that cave continues for more than a week or two, though, it's time for more gentle digging to figure out what's truly going on inside his head.

Clue #3: He sleeps until you're out the door, but then you return at lunch and he's happily munching and gaming, still in his sweats. He gives you that "uh-oh" look that he did when his hand was caught in the cookie jar when he was eight. Now you know your son got sick of school and all the work involved and decided he'd give himself a vacation.

If this is the case, here's how I would proceed.

"Looks like you're enjoying gaming. It's good to play games for a break, but this is school time. Since you're not going to school, I have some jobs for you to do during the time you'd be there. There's plenty to do around here, so I'll have no problem assigning you some work to replace your school time."

"Work? What do you mean, work?" he says. Now his attention is on you, not the game.

"Oh, I need the basement walls painted. I think a light yellow would be nice and sunny, don't you?" You smile. "Now that you're available during the day, we might as well get that done. We've been talking about it for a long time. And then there's . . ." And you proceed to talk about a long list of house projects that you know he'd absolutely hate doing because they're boring.

Then you say, "Since you're no longer in school, it makes sense for you to get a real job. I see that the convenience store down the block is hiring. Oh, wait, you have to be 16 to work there. It'll be tougher to get a good-paying job if you're not at least a high-school graduate. And since you're not in school, you could look for an apartment of your own . . . but you have to be 18 to sign for it." You shrug. "All that's up to you, though. It certainly looks like you've got your work cut out for you. I'll make up a list of to-dos around here and leave it on the counter tomorrow morning. I'm so glad you'll be able to tackle it."

Then you walk off, leaving your son staring at you open-mouthed.

This vacation from school thing isn't going like he'd planned. Likely he'll decide that getting out the door to school tomorrow is a much better option.

Case solved, Dr. Watson.

Sensitive Child

Q: Our six-year-old is unusually sensitive. She needs set routines and gets very upset if anything changes. We end up placating her or tiptoeing around her. We've even changed plans. She cried when my wife and I tried to leave for a date night, and we had to stay home.

Sometimes it feels like she's in control instead of us. Any advice about how to deal with such a sensitive child? This is getting crazy. I need some time alone with my wife.

A: Any time parents tell me about a "sensitive" child, I know immediately they have a powerful child. Power comes in all kinds of sizes, shapes, and packages. If she is manipulating you by making you walk on eggshells around her, she's indeed controlling both of you.

Who gave her that power in the first place? Did you try to keep things quiet when she was sleeping as a baby so she wasn't disturbed? Did you always make sure she was comfortable? Did you do things for her that she could do for herself?

If so, she discovered early on that she can make the planets revolve in her home by a mere stretch of her fingers and her vocal cords. In short, she understands exactly how to make you do what she wants you to do. She didn't want you two to leave without

240

her, so she had a cry fest to change your mind. And you did, so she won.

Right now your sensitive child is certain she's at the center of the universe. But what happens when she gets out into the wide world and figures out she's not?

It's time for you and your wife to go on that date night tonight. Get Grandma, Grandpa, your sister, or a sitter to babysit. Make sure they are clued in on what you're doing and why, so they don't make unnecessary phone calls to you. And it's only fair that they know the situation so they're prepared for all the emotion that goes with it.

> *Right now your sensitive child is certain she's at the center of the universe. But what happens when she gets out into the wide world and figures out she's not?*

As you put on your coat to go out that door, tears will start to flow. Remember one thing: You want this misbehavior to change, right? Then *you* have to change.

What did you say in the past? "Oh, honey, don't cry. We won't be gone that long. Mommy and Daddy sometimes need time by ourselves. We'll see you soon."

Did that work? No, it only accelerated the crying, and panic ensued. You felt terrible and couldn't walk out the door.

So what will you do this time? Lean down and say, "Have a fun time with Grandma. We'll see you tomorrow when you wake up."

Then you proceed straight out that door and do not return until your date is over. You put your phone on silent and refuse to answer any calls. You have a real date with your wife.

When you get home, your daughter may look flushed from crying, but she'll be asleep in bed. She had dose number one of her lesson that she's not number one in the universe.

Better now than when she's 21, don't you think?

Entitled Kids

Q: Why is it that every time my kids misbehave, I'm the one who feels guilty?

I cook my younger daughter's favorite dinner, and she changes her mind as soon as I put it in front of her. "Mom, why did you make this? I *hate* this." But last week she downed two plates of it.

And when my son yells at me for something I didn't get done, even though I did five other things for him that day, I'm the one who walks away feeling bad.

Then there's my older daughter. I do her laundry twice a week, and still she complains, "Mom, I have nothing to wear, and it's *your fault.*"

Sometimes I feel like going on strike. Would that be too out of line for a mom?

A: I think you hit on the perfect solution all by yourself. If I were you, I'd go on strike for at least two weeks. Without you, your kids won't have dinners that aren't out of a box or can. Nobody else will do all the errands that matter mostly to them. And they won't have anyone who will pick up their dirty laundry strewn across their bedroom floors and clean it for them like magic.

Your kids are entitled. They think they deserve everything you do for them, and then some. But all those things you're describing aren't rights; they're privileges. Tons of moms I know no longer cook at all. They don't do many errands for their kids. And they certainly don't feel they have to do the laundry. Your kids need to experience a week or two without the perks that you bring to their lives, and then they'll feel a bit more grateful.

But here's what you don't do. You don't forewarn them. You don't announce, "Hey, kids, you're driving me crazy, so I'm not going to do a thing for you for the next two weeks." Instead, you don't make breakfast. Their sack lunches for school aren't ready on the counter. When they get home from school, there are no fresh-baked out-of-a-tube cookies on a plate. There's no food at dinner time.

You are MIA for at least the first couple of days when they're home. You spend long-awaited evenings with girlfriends or other family members. You're not easily reachable by cell. You sleep in those mornings and marvel at the wonder of it.

Those kids are going to discover dinner from a can and will have to learn the effort it takes to create those bag lunches they turn their noses up at. The day will come when their favorite outfits are . . . guess what? In the laundry and not available. The errands will stack up, and they might

> *Your kids need to experience a week or two without the perks that you bring to their lives, and then they'll feel a bit more grateful.*

have to walk to a nearby store with money from their piggy bank to get that purple T-shirt they need for purple day at school.

This is what I call "the bread-and-water treatment" for entitled children.

After a week or two (depending on the age of your children and how engrained the entitlement is), you can step back in. But be careful about assuming all of your old tasks. Otherwise they will think you only went temporarily crazy and have turned back into the mom they know who will do anything for them.

So you make dinner one night, but you don't the next. When they ask, "Hey, where's dinner?" you say, "Oh, I didn't feel like making it tonight," while flipping this book's pages.

"So what are we supposed to eat?" they ask.

You wave a hand. "Whatever you feel like. I'm sure you'll come up with something."

A few rounds of that and not doing the laundry, and those kids will have a new appreciation of ol' Mom. After all, Mom does make the world go round, even if her kids don't always know it.

Caught Cheating

Q: My high-schooler was caught cheating on a science test. I'm so embarrassed. I can't believe it's my kid. He usually gets top grades, so why would he do that? I don't even know what to say to him, much less what to do. Of our four kids, he's the good and easy one. This seems way out of left field.

If this were your kid, what would you do?

A: Well, academic cheating isn't exactly breaking news. It's been around since Cain and Abel took their first tests, I think. In fact, in one widespread college cheating scandal in 2019, more than 50 adults were caught red-handed, including coaches, test administrators, CEOs, and Hollywood celebrities . . . not to mention the scandal embarrassed the heck out of elite universities like Yale, Stanford, Georgetown, USC, and UCLA.[6]

But when it hits home instead of the newsstand, it's a whole different story.

Your high-schooler is already embarrassed enough by his actions and knows he has royally disappointed you. The best thing you can do at this point is give him some time to process and give yourself some time to regroup your thoughts.

The next day, you might say, "The cheating incident is now water under the bridge. We will move on from here and not wallow in it. But there's one thing I would like to know when you want to share it: *why* you felt that cheating was the best option."

Then you wait until he's unscrambled his thoughts. It may be a day or two, or more. When he does talk, do what is hard for all parents to do: shut your mouth and listen. Some of what he says may not be easy for you to hear. If he's been your good, top-grade, hardworking son, he may have cracked under the pressure of always having to be that. Maybe science isn't his thing. Maybe he was worried about his GPA to get into college. Maybe he didn't want to disappoint you by not meeting your expectations. Maybe he saw what he thought was an easy way out and made a bad decision. Again, all of these are common reasons for top students to consider cheating. This time the lure was too strong, and he took the bait.

However hard the facts may be, it's time that you hear them and your son voices them. Better now in high school, where the ante is not as high as it would be in college or later in life.

Yes, you're disappointed, but anger or the ice treatment won't resolve anything. Instead, say something like, "I'm sorry that you felt like you were under such pressure that you had to cheat to make a good grade. That action has certainly backfired. Your mom and I were surprised, disappointed, and embarrassed when the school called us in to talk about the cheating. I know we expect a lot out of you, but there's something else I want you to know."

You see your son clench his fists, waiting for the hammer blow.

Instead, you say gently, "For us, you don't have to be anyone but yourself. You don't have to be good at every subject. I know science isn't your thing. We'd have been happy with a C. I'm sorry we've pressured you so much to meet our expectations. We believe in you and in your abilities. Who you are—kind, courteous, generous, and helpful at home—is far more than we could have dreamed in a son.

"Going back to school after this, with the other kids knowing, isn't going to be easy. But you need to finish out your year there. Whenever you need to talk, I'm here."

Then you close the book on the cheating and give your son what you'd long for—a second chance. You never dig up those bones from the backyard again.

Believe me, he's learned a lesson he won't forget in his lifetime.

Sibling Fights and Tattling

Q: My kids fight like cats and dogs. Really, they do, almost 24/7. When you have five of them, the noise can be deafening. When they're not fighting, they're tattling on each other. If you ever saw me, I'd be the super-tired-looking mom with bags under her eyes, since my two oldest fight even at midnight. My two youngest wake me up early in the morning to tattle on each other.

I'm tired of being the referee. How can I stop this constant battling and tattling in my home?

A: Simple. Just remove yourself from your children's wind. When they start tussling, say, "I'm sure you can handle it between the two of you," and walk away. Preferably go into a room where you can't see or hear them (at least much) and lock the door. Or go out for a drive, get yourself some coffee or a treat, and linger for a while.

If you're not there to tattle to, the tattling loses its punch. Your new favorite lines should be, "Oh, really? Well, if your sister did that, then she can tell me herself. I don't need to hear it from you." Or, better yet, march that kid right over to the other kid and say, "Sarah, Amanda has something she wants to tell you." That tactic usually ends the whole tattling scene. How do I know? Because I've seen it work.

> Remove yourself from your children's wind.

When I was assistant dean of students, I handled all kinds of disciplinary problems with college students. But the staff was the hardest to deal with. One of them would show up at my door and say, "Uh, Dr. Leman, can I talk to you for a minute?"

Dumb me. I opened the door and said, "Sure. Come on in and sit down."

Forty minutes later I was thinking, *Why, why, why? All she's talking about is how bad the other secretaries are.*

The next time she showed up, I wasn't so dumb. "Cindy, I'm so glad you came in," I said with a smile. "Would you come with me, please?"

We walked right over to the secretary she was complaining about. I said, "Barb, Cindy has something to tell you." Then I shut up and stood there.

Cindy's response was interesting. She gave a small shrug, looking embarrassed, and said quietly, "Well, it's not really a big thing, but I was wondering if . . ."

Handling the situation directly by connecting the complainer and the person she complained about worked like a charm. Word spread swiftly that I'd do the same thing to anyone who tattled. Case solved.

Why don't you try this with your kids and see what happens? It's all about holding them accountable for their words.

Above all, don't get dragged back in. Refuse to referee. Let them handle the fight all by themselves. It's amazing how fast fights will end if the kids are on their own. They usually feel fairly stupid. Or they might come up with a surprising solution they hadn't thought of before because they were too focused on vying for your attention.

If all fails, buy some of those big, soft boxing gloves. Five pairs—one for each kid—would be a good investment, don't you think? Then let them have a round with each other in the garage. That can be your "fight zone" to resolve problems. It ought to wear them out physically too, so they'll sleep. Then *you* can get some well-deserved sleep.

Wishing you lots of z's . . .

Habitual Liar and Rebel

Q: Wow, this is hard to say, but my kid seems to be a habitual liar. When he was young, he told imaginative stories that stretched the truth. A fish he caught that was five inches long suddenly became an 18-incher. We used to laugh.

But now we're no longer laughing. I can't trust my 17-year-old to ever be where he says he is. I've caught him time and time again in a lie. Last week he lied about being at a school event when he was at a club with a fake ID. We only found out the truth because he'd passed out from drinking too much and two of his supposed new friends dumped him in front of our house before racing off in their Jeep.

I grew up in a family where honesty and integrity were extremely important. My son seems to be going the other direction. What did I do wrong? Why is my son like this? And what can I do about it?

A: Some kids will wander. But there are ways to rein him in, especially since he's still under 18.

If you've strongly stressed honesty and integrity, he might be tired of hearing about it, especially if you've lectured him on those topics. Or perhaps he thinks your words don't match your actions.

But here is what I think is at play. I'm going to guess that he's your middle son and that your older son is a perfect shooting star. Your middle son has no way of catching that star or competing with it, so he's running in the other direction. He's *making* you pay attention to him with his misbehavior. *Maybe if I'm bad enough, they'll notice that I actually exist.*

It's easy for parents to assume that one brother will be like the other. Not so. In fact, the opposite is true in birth order. The second son usually goes the complete opposite direction of the first. It's his way of saying, "I'm me, not my brother."

But if your 17-year-old is drinking—in fact, so much that he passes out—and he has the family car sometimes, it is definitely time to intervene.

Wait until his hangover abates, but don't shush your other kids. In fact, let them make as much noise as possible. When your middle son doesn't look as bleary-eyed, throw this little statement his way: "Well, that was a new experience. Seeing my son tossed out onto the lawn like a landed fish."

He starts to fidget. "Uh, well . . ."

"You'll soon be 18. And we've never expected you to be your brother because you're you."

He stares at you. *Where is Dad going with this?*

"What you decide to make of yourself, and the way you decide to live, will increasingly be more your business. If that's how you want to spend your nights and the morning after, it's your life. You'll do what you want to do. But you are still a part of our family and always will be. That means you're a Kranz. You represent our family. But most of all, you represent yourself. If that is how you choose to live—lying about where you are, drinking, and ending up on our front lawn at midnight—then it's time for you to look for a new home. Your little brother and little sister are still here in our home, and they look up to you. It's not fair for them to see such behavior, or to have other kids snickering about their brother at school.

"You graduate in two months. You should start looking for a job and an apartment now. Let's set the date of June 15 for you to be out of the house."

"But Dad, what about college?" he asks, panicked. "Don't you want me to go to college?"

You tilt your head. "Do you think that investing in college for you is an appropriate option right now, given your activities?"

He hangs his head. "Well, no."

"Then June 15 it is."

The discussion ends, and your son, who expected grounding, is stunned.

Sometimes a parent's gotta do what he's gotta do. He has to shake up his kid until common sense settles in. And if that doesn't do it, seeing how much an apartment costs and how difficult it is to get a job will.

> Sometimes a parent's gotta do what he's gotta do. He has to shake up his kid until common sense settles in.

Is this hard to do as a parent? Yes, it's incredibly hard. But parenting sometimes calls for tough decisions like this one. If you can't be tough this time, your 17-year-old might be the 37-year-old who still lives in your basement suite and parties, because he's never been forced to become an adult.

So carry on with your bon voyage. It's the only way to force the transformation that often happens when rebellion meets real-life responsibilities.

Texting, Gaming, and YouTube Addicts

Q: My kids are constantly on their phones. The few times we do manage to have dinner, I look around the table and I might as well be alone. Even my husband is answering work emails. I spend a lot of time on my phone myself, but at least I try not to answer my cell when it's a family dinner. I've said things like, "Hey, kids, dinner's when we should be talking, not texting," but it gets me nowhere. I only get the "Seriously, Mom?" expression or the ever-present eye roll.

When they aren't on their phones, they're on their computers, watching YouTube videos, gaming, or listening to music with their earbuds in. One day it hit me. The reason we don't have any time to connect as a family is because of all this technology. That comes first, before family.

How can I turn this around so we can reconnect, without starting World War III in my house by taking their electronics?

A: You and your family need a month on a desert island with no technology and those little fruity drinks with the miniature umbrellas. But since that's not likely to happen for most families, here's where I'd start.

Any change has to start with you and your husband. So talk to him about your concerns, and agree together not to bring your cell phones to your next family dinner. Instead, bring up interesting pieces of news and ask for your kids' opinions. For example, "Every year we do a family vacation. Usually Dad and I decide where to go, but this year we want to know what you guys think and where you'd like to go."

That ought to get the conversation moving. If they don't respond and don't get off their phones, then say, "I really miss talking to you guys, since you're important to me. But since we're always on our phones, even at dinner, I'd like to try something different for a month. See that basket right by the dining room door? On Mondays and Thursdays, we'll turn off our cell phones and leave them in that basket during dinner. That's only two hours a week. I think we could all do that, don't you?"

You'll get some mutterings, but when you put it that way, it's tough for them to say no. Those kids who act as if they don't like you or aren't interested really do want to please you.

Two family dinners a week where you actually converse about things that matter is a small but important start to more meaningful family interactions. At the next family dinner, there will likely be silent, awkward moments. People who are used to texting instead of talking often don't know what to say.

Asking your children questions, such as, "So, Tommy, how was your day today?" will get you nowhere.

Ditto with, "I know you have a history paper due soon, Angie. What's it on?" Instead, come prepared with ideas. "I saw a fun video yesterday about a guy who helped save a miniature donkey that otherwise wouldn't have lived, and now it lives indoors with him and follows him around like a pet dog."

Kid 1: "Oh yeah, I saw that. There's another one about a goose that got hurt as a baby. A man saved him and later trained him how to fly. He took the bird out on his speedboat, held the bird up, and floored it."

Kid 2: "That's cool. I wanna see that. Would you show me after dinner?"

Kid 1: "Sure. There are all sorts of great animal videos like that. I watch them all the time. Did you know that a Canada goose can . . ."

> Asking your children questions, such as, "So, Tommy, how was your day today?" will get you nowhere.

And you're off and running with two siblings who, 20 minutes ago, said they couldn't stand each other. See how easy that was? Bet it wouldn't take much to gather the family around a computer screen to watch some of those animal videos together, now that you know they're interested.

Or throw this out at the dinner table: "I'd love your opinion on something. There have been a lot of shocking news stories about really rich people who paid a lot of money to get their kids into the right college. We're not rich, but if we were and I did that for the two of you, how would you feel about it?"

Wait for it. If you have two kids, their responses will predictably be as different as night and day.

Kid 1: "I'd be upset and hurt. You don't believe in me very much, do you? I mean, you paid somebody because you didn't think I could get in myself by studying and working hard."

Kid 2 (shrugs): "If I could get into a big school like that as a done deal, without sweating over an application or a test, cool! What's bad about that?"

Kid 1: "*You* didn't get into the school, Dumbo. Mom got you into it by paying somebody. You're telling me you'd feel good about that?"

Kid 2: (Silence.)

Kid 1: "And you'd get caught because you're stupid. Even if you didn't, you could never keep up with the work at a college you didn't deserve to get into."

Look at that. With no lecture from you, your older son has solidified his belief in the self-reward of working hard, and your younger daughter got a wake-up call about the real world.

There are a few hills in your parenting journey worth trudging up and staking your flag on, and family time is one of them. After all, 10 years from now, who will still be in their lives: the friend who betrayed them a month later, the colleague they worked with for a year, or the family members sitting right around this dinner table?

I'd also like to suggest you plan a family activity every two weeks. Make it a no-miss event and do something fun. Go to the beach on a Saturday, drive bumper cars for an afternoon, have a picnic, splash each other in the sprinkler in the backyard, go skating, go skiing, go bowling, make snow angels, wash the family car(s) in the driveway, cook a new ethnic dish with everyone helping, watch some crazy or sweet animal videos . . . The only limit is your imagination. Engage your kids' interest by saying, "I'd love to hear your ideas for things we can do and places we can go." The family that plays together stays together.

> *There are a few hills in your parenting journey worth trudging up and staking your flag on, and family time is one of them.*

Initially kids will grumble about anything that doesn't immediately give them what they want (like the ability to answer urgent texts from friends that say, "Whatcha doin'?"), but they'll come around. Those two family dinners without electronics will set a routine, and kids thrive on routine. Most families who follow this technique for a while discover that even on the nights they don't have to put their phones in the basket, the kids put them there automatically and engage in conversation when they sit down.

Eventually, you might even hear them say what one mom heard her 17-year-old daughter say to a friend: "No, I'm not available on Friday nights." Why? Because that was the night she gamed with her dad and had conversations about life. See? Even that gaming you hate can be used for the good purpose of growing your relationship with your child, if you take advantage of her interest.

Ditto with watching videos on YouTube and listening to songs on iTunes. Simply drop a comment: "That song you're listening to is intriguing. If there's a music video out, I'd love for you to show me sometime." Even kids who act like they don't want you in their world *love* to share the videos they're watching and songs they're listening to, especially when you're asking and not demanding.

Another tip: When you do watch those videos and see the song lyrics, find *something positive* to say even if you hated them. "The choreography is simply amazing . . . so filled with energy." Then you add what will capture your child's attention and heart: "I'd love to know how you found that group, what you know about them, and anything else you'd want to tell me." By doing so, you engage with your child in her world.

If you show an open rather than a judgmental attitude toward all the influences in her world, she's more likely to say, "Hey, Mom, I put a couple of new videos in my Watch Later playlist. You want to watch them with me tonight after I finish my homework?"

From watching YouTube videos that interest her, you'll see what issues and topics she's passionate about, hear her thoughts about boys and life, and learn much, much more. As topics come up, do some googling yourself on those points of interest to establish natural, ongoing conversation.

"Hey, you told me that the lead singer of that group is big on supporting organizations in the poorest parts of Rio de Janeiro. I came across a cool online article about it yesterday."

Your daughter turns toward you. "Really? Where is it?" She hops online, and the two of you look at the article together and discuss it.

A month later she comes to you and says, "I did a bunch of research on those organizations and found one I'd like to show you. Would you and Dad be open to me working there in Rio for a month after graduation? If I could save up the money for the airfare and most of my living expenses while I'm there?"

Don't underestimate the power of YouTube in introducing globalization to your children. Nor should you underestimate the long-term value of your teenager seeing how disadvantaged people live halfway across the planet. There's nothing that takes away entitlement and increases gratefulness more than meeting real people who show joy in finding clean water and having two meals of rice and beans a day.

Taking phones and computers away from kids as a punishment for their overuse is not the answer today to creating more family time. It only fuels resentment and the concepts that Mom and Dad are prehistoric dinosaurs and don't get the real world.

> *Taking phones and computers away from kids only fuels resentment.*

Instead, introduce the idea and practice that it is *possible and good* to unplug sometimes, like two nights a week during family dinners and on that biweekly family outing. Then step into your child's world, using their passion for gaming, internet surfing, listening to iTunes, and watching YouTube, to discover and explore their interests.

Changing your kids' misbehaviors starts with changing your own parenting techniques. If you want kids who have the potential to unplug, then model unplugging sometimes yourself.

Enjoy those family dinners and outings while you can. Cell phones and computers will still be around in five years, but your kids may not still be in your nest.

Making family time a priority is the right thing to do.

Notes

1. Eva Dreikurs Ferguson, *Adlerian Theory: An Introduction* (CreateSpace, 2009), 4–7.

2. "Imprinting and Relationships," *Psychologist World*, accessed March 30, 2019, https://www.psychologistworld.com/developmental/imprinting-lorenz-filial-sexual.

3. Anne Ortlund, *Children Are Wet Cement* (Grand Rapids: Revell, 1981).

4. "Kevin Leman: Who's Controlling Whom?" CBN.com, accessed March 30, 2019, https://www1.cbn.com/family/kevin-leman%3A-who%27s-controlling-whom%3F.

5. Don Dinkmeyer and Gary McKay, "Goals of Misbehavior," PedagoNet.com, accessed March 30, 2019, http://www.pedagonet.com/other/MISB.htm.

6. Madeline Holcombe, "USC Says Students Connected to Cheating Scheme Will Be Denied Admission," CNN, March 14, 2019, https://www.cnn.com/2019/03/13/us/college-admission-cheating-scheme-wednesday/index.html.

About Dr. Kevin Leman

An internationally known psychologist, radio and television personality, speaker, educator, and humorist, **Dr. Kevin Leman** has taught and entertained audiences worldwide with his wit and commonsense psychology.

The *New York Times* bestselling and award-winning author of over 50 titles, including *The Birth Order Book*, *Making Children Mind without Losing Yours*, *Have a New Kid by Friday*, and *Sheet Music*, has made thousands of house calls through radio and television programs, including *FOX & Friends*, Hallmark Channel's *Home & Family*, *The View*, FOX's *The Morning Show*, *Today*, *Morning in America*, *The 700 Club*, CBS's *The Early Show*, CNN, and *Focus on the Family*. Dr. Leman has served as a contributing family psychologist to *Good Morning America* and frequently speaks to schools, CEO groups, and businesses, including Fortune 500 companies and others such as YPO, Million Dollar Round Table, and Top of the Table.

Dr. Leman's professional affiliations include the American Psychological Association, SAG-AFTRA, and the North American Society of Adlerian Psychology. He received the Distinguished Alumnus Award (1993) and an honorary Doctor of Humane

Letters degree (2010) from North Park University; and a bachelor's degree in psychology, and later his master's and doctorate degrees, as well as the Alumni Achievement Award (2003), from the University of Arizona. Dr. Leman is the founder and chairman of the board of Leman Academy of Excellence (www.leman academy.com).

Originally from Williamsville, New York, Dr. Leman and his wife, Sande, live in Tucson, Arizona, and have five children and four grandchildren.

If you're looking for an entertaining speaker for your event or fund-raiser, or for information regarding business consultations, webinars, or the annual "Wit and Wisdom" cruise, please contact:

Dr. Kevin Leman
PO Box 35370
Tucson, Arizona 85740
Phone: (520) 797-3830
Fax: (520) 797-3809
www.birthorderguy.com
www.drleman.com

Follow Dr. Kevin Leman on Facebook (facebook.com/DrKevin Leman) and on Twitter (@DrKevinLeman). Check out the free podcasts at birthorderguy.com/podcast.

Resources by Dr. Kevin Leman

Nonfiction Books for Adults

The Birth Order Book
Have a New Kid by Friday
Why Your Kids Misbehave—and What to Do about It
When Your Kid Is Hurting
Planet Middle School
The Intimate Connection
Sheet Music
Have a New Husband by Friday
Have a New Teenager by Friday
Have a New You by Friday
Have a New Sex Life by Friday
Have a Happy Family by Friday
The Way of the Shepherd (written with William Pentak)
The Way of the Wise
Be the Dad She Needs You to Be
What a Difference a Mom Makes
Parenting the Powerful Child
Under the Sheets

Making Children Mind without Losing Yours
It's Your Kid, Not a Gerbil!
Born to Win
7 Things He'll Never Tell You . . . But You Need to Know
What Your Childhood Memories Say about You
Running the Rapids
Becoming the Parent God Wants You to Be
Becoming a Couple of Promise
A Chicken's Guide to Talking Turkey with Your Kids about Sex (written with Kathy Flores Bell)
First-Time Mom
Step-parenting 101
Living in a Stepfamily without Getting Stepped On
The Perfect Match
Be Your Own Shrink
Stopping Stress before It Stops You
Single Parenting That Works
Why Your Best Is Good Enough
Smart Women Know When to Say No

Fiction: The Worthington Destiny Series, with Jeff Nesbit

A Perfect Ambition
A Powerful Secret
A Primary Decision

Books for Children, with Kevin Leman II

My Firstborn, There's No One Like You
My Middle Child, There's No One Like You
My Youngest, There's No One Like You
My Only Child, There's No One Like You

My Adopted Child, There's No One Like You
My Grandchild, There's No One Like You

DVD/Video Series for Group Use

Have a New Kid by Friday
Making Children Mind without Losing Yours (parenting edition)
Making Children Mind without Losing Yours (public school teacher edition)
Value-Packed Parenting
Making the Most of Marriage
Running the Rapids
Single Parenting That Works
Bringing Peace and Harmony to the Blended Family

DVDs for Home Use

Straight Talk on Parenting
Why You Are the Way You Are
Have a New Husband by Friday
Have a New You by Friday
Have a New Kid by Friday

Available at 1-800-770-3830 • www.birthorderguy.com • www.drleman.com

Visit BirthOrderGuy.com
for more information, resources, and videos
from Dr. Kevin Leman's popular books.

Follow Dr. Leman on

 Dr Kevin Leman

drleman

Discover MORE Content from
DR. KEVIN LEMAN

Tune in to his weekly podcast

Have a New Kid by Friday
PODCAST

DR. KEVIN LEMAN

Available wherever you get your podcasts

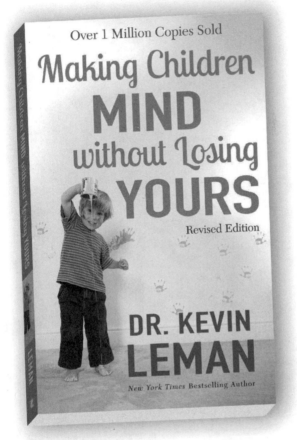

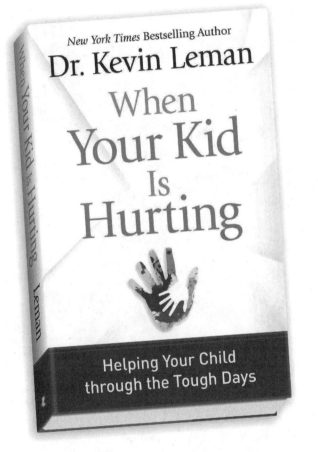

Powerful kids don't just happen . . .
THEY'RE CREATED.

Whether loud and temperamental, quiet and sensitive, or stubborn and manipulative, powerful children can make living with them a challenge. But it doesn't have to be that way.